Heinemann Explore Science

Pupil Book 4

CW01594522

Randal Cremer Primary School
Ormsby Street
London E2 8JG
Tel: 020 7739 8162
Fax: 020 7729 5807

Tara Lievesley • Deborah Herridge
Series editor John Stringer

Heinemann

Author team
Deborah Herridge and Tara Lievesley

Series editor
John Stringer

Acknowledgements
The publishers wish to thank the following for permission to reproduce photographs:
Front cover photograph: **Zefa**
Back cover photographs: **Oxford Scientific Films** (top), **Science Photo Library** (centre and bottom), **Photodisc** (centre left)

The Art Archive – page 24; **Trevor Clifford** – pages 36 (bottom), 44 (bottom), 79 (bottom), 81, 82 (top and centre); **Digital Stock** – page 20 (bottom); **Jeff Edwards** – page 44 (top); **Peter Gould** – pages 34 (top), 45; **Image Select** – page 68 (centre); **Inklines & Small House** – page 15; **Andrew Lambert** – pages 36 (top), 57; **Mary Evans Picture Library** – page 23; **Zul Mukhida** – page 19 (bottom); **Oxford Scientific Films** – pages 13, 14 (top), 27, 29, 30, 31, 56; **Philip Parkhouse** – page 82 (bottom); **Photodisc** – page 12 (bottom); **Science Photo Library** – pages 6 (top), 8, 33, 34 (bottom), 49 (bottom), 54 (bottom), 62 (top), 68 (top); **Stockfile** – page 17; **Ed Stuart** – page 14 (bottom); **Tony Stone Images** – page 6 (bottom); **Wildlife Matters** – pages 22 (top), 32

Heinemann Educational Publishers
Halley Court, Jordan Hill, Oxford, OX2 8EJ
a division of Harcourt Education Ltd
www.heinemann.co.uk

Heinemann is a registered trademark of Harcourt Education Ltd

© Harcourt Education Ltd 2003.

This book is copyright and reproduction of the whole or part without the publisher's written permission is prohibited.

First published 2003

06 05
10 9 8 7 6 5 4 3 2
ISBN 0 435 133918 / 978 0 435 133917

Designed and typeset by **Day1**
Illustrated by **Andy Hamilton, Shelagh McNicholas, Jon Stuart and Chrome Dome Design**
Printed in Spain by **Edelvives, Zaragoza**

Contents

How to use this book

At the beginning of each unit there is a list of things you should already know or be able to do.

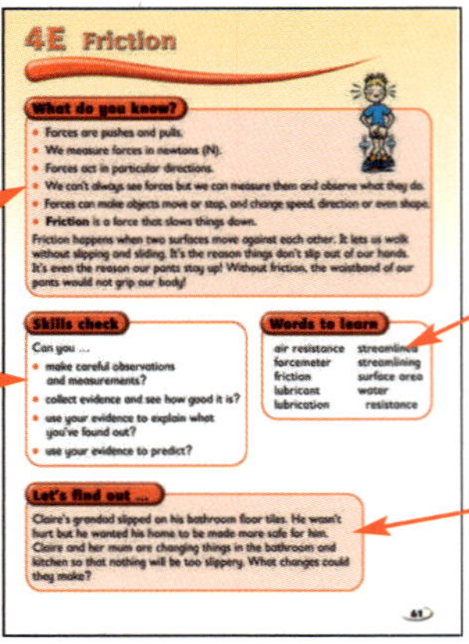

This shows words in the unit that are important. Try to remember them.

Think about this question. By the end of the unit you will know how to answer it.

This box tells you what the lesson is about.

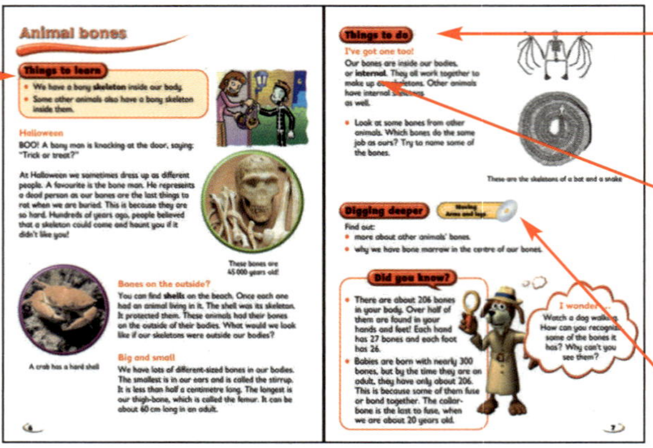

Try these activities. Your teacher will help you.

Find out what words in bold mean in the glossary at the back of the book.

Use a CD-ROM to find out more. The colour shows which CD to use – **Life Processes**, **Materials** or **Physical Processes**.

This box tells you what you will find out during the lesson. Your teacher will help you.

Look out for safety tips!

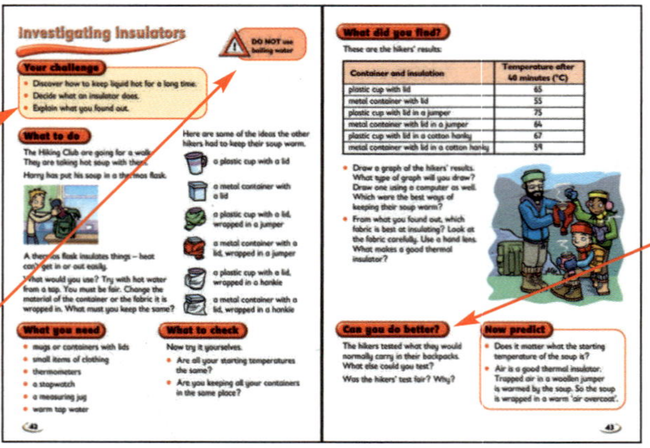

Use what you have learned to answer these questions.

Check what you have learned in each unit.

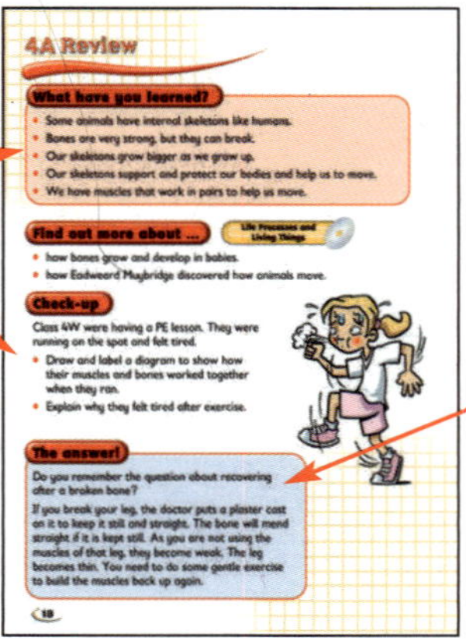

Now answer the first question.

4A Moving and growing

What do you know?

- You can name some parts of your body.
- We need to eat to grow and be healthy.
- As we get older we grow bigger.

What would we be like without any bones? We would not be able to stand – or move! Our skeleton provides us with a way to move and keep upright, and it also **protects** us. It doesn't stay the same size though, or we would never grow any taller than a baby.

Skills check

Can you …

- compare observations that you make?
- decide what to investigate and collect the evidence?
- say what your evidence means?
- use a ruler to measure length?

Words to learn

contract	protection	skull
external	relax	spine
flexible	ribs	support
internal	shell	tendon
muscle	skeleton	vertebrate

Let's find out …

If you break your leg, a doctor puts a plaster cast on it. When the cast comes off, your leg is often much thinner than it was. Why does the doctor put the cast on? Why is your leg thinner? How have the **muscles** changed? What can you do to make both legs look the same again?

Animal bones

Things to learn

- We have a bony **skeleton** inside our body.
- Some other animals also have a bony skeleton inside them.

Halloween

BOO! A bony man is knocking at the door, saying: "Trick or treat?"

At Halloween we sometimes dress up as different people. A favourite is the bone man. He represents a dead person as our bones are the last things to rot when we are buried. This is because they are so hard. Hundreds of years ago, people believed that a skeleton could come and haunt you if it didn't like you!

These bones are 45 000 years old!

A crab has a hard shell

Bones on the outside?

You can find **shells** on the beach. Once each one had an animal living in it. The shell was its skeleton. It protected them. These animals had their bones on the outside of their bodies. What would we look like if our skeletons were outside our bodies?

Big and small

We have lots of different-sized bones in our bodies. The smallest is in our ears and is called the stirrup. It is less than half a centimetre long. The longest is our thigh-bone, which is called the femur. It can be about 60 cm long in an adult.

Things to do

I've got one too!

Our bones are inside our bodies, or **internal**. They all work together to make up our skeletons. Other animals have internal skeletons as well.

- Look at some bones from other animals. Which bones do the same job as ours? Try to name some of the bones.

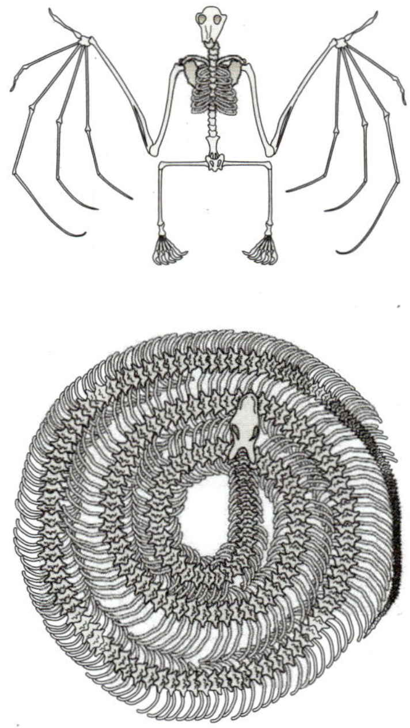

These are the skeletons of a bat and a snake

Digging deeper

Moving
Arms and legs

Find out:

- more about other animals' bones.
- why we have bone marrow in the centre of our bones.

Did you know?

- There are about 206 bones in your body. Over half of them are found in your hands and feet! Each hand has 27 bones and each foot has 26.
- Babies are born with nearly 300 bones, but by the time they are an adult, they have only about 206. This is because some of them fuse or bond together. The collar-bone is the last to fuse, when we are about 20 years old.

I wonder ...

Watch a dog walking. How can you recognize some of the bones it has? Why can't you see them?

Broken bones

Things to learn

- Descriptions of the appearance and feel of bones.
- Names of some important bones in the body.
- Bones need to be strong, but can break.

A dog's dinner

Dogs eat the bones of other animals. They contain a soft, tasty core called bone marrow. But chicken bones are brittle and splinter easily and can hurt the insides of a dog's throat.

Humpty Dumpty ...

Our bones are very similar to eggshell. They are made with some of the same substance. It is also found in teeth. It is called calcium. Bones are very strong, until you give them a hard, sudden knock. Then they break, just like Humpty Dumpty falling off the wall!

Couldn't put Humpty together again!

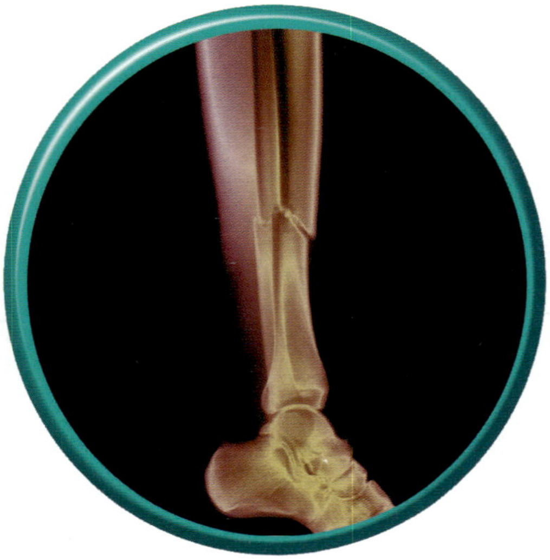

Find the break in this leg bone

From outer space?

X-rays are not from outer space. They were discovered over 100 years ago, by Wilhelm Röntgen. He used them to look through his wife's hand. He could see her bones. X-rays pass through your flesh, but are stopped by your bones.

Things to do

The ankle-bone is connected to the ...

- How many bones can you name? Your **ribs**, **skull**, or **backbone**? Label them on a diagram of the skeleton.
- Name all the bones you can.

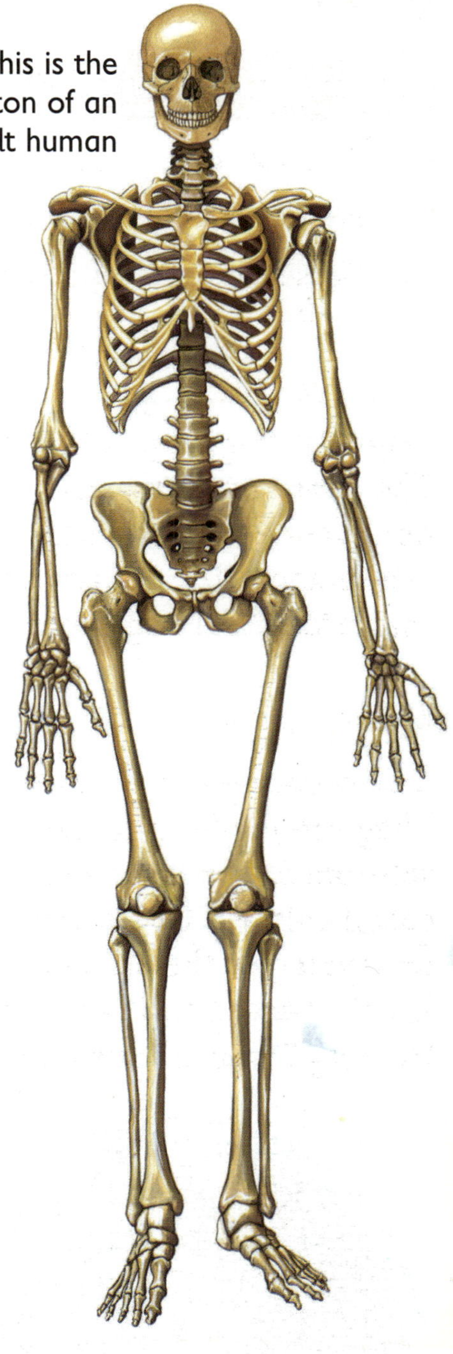

This is the skeleton of an adult human

Digging deeper

Moving
Breaks and sprains

Find out:

- more about how bones break.
- how bones mend themselves.

I wonder ...

What did Jack and Jill use vinegar and brown paper for? What do doctors use instead?

Did you know?

- Young chickens have a soft breastbone. It hardens with calcium as the chicken gets older. If you eat a young chicken, you can see the soft, flexible breastbone.
- Your knuckles crack because pulling on them quickly makes a vacuum in the joints. Fluid rushes into the spaces, making a popping sound.

Growing bones

Your challenge

- Find out if our skeletons grow when we do.
- Measure lengths accurately.
- Decide if the evidence supports your ideas.

What to do

Class 4 want to see if bones get bigger as we grow. They have decided to measure bones on themselves, some children from Class 3 and Class 5, their teacher and their learning assistant. They are not sure how much evidence to collect. Here are some of their suggestions.
Which do you think is best?

What you need

- rulers or tape measures

What to check

Now try it yourselves.

- What are you going to measure?
- What will you keep the same to make it a fair test?
- Who will have the biggest bones? Can you explain why?

What did you find?

The children in Class 4 decided to measure the forearms of everyone they could. Here are some of their measurements.

Name	Length of forearm (cm)
Emily (age 7)	13
Jared (age 8)	15
Kirsten (age 9)	18
Miss Shepherd	23
Mr Davis	25

- What kind of chart can you produce of Class 4's results? Try it by hand, then use a computer to draw it.
- What does your chart show? Which person had the longest bones? Why do you think that was? Does this prove your idea?

Can you do better?

Did you measure accurately?

How would you change the way you collected your evidence?

Are their any other questions you could ask?

Now predict

Class 4E are also trying to find out if your bones grow when you get older. They have decided just to measure all the forearms of their classmates.

- How would you show them that there is a better way to collect the evidence? What is wrong with their idea?
- Class 4W have decided to measure both the leg bones and forearms of their classmates. Can you say what they will find out? How will their evidence be different from Class 4E's?

Your skeleton

Things to learn

- Your skeleton supports your body.
- Some animals have other ways of supporting their bodies.

Blob of jelly

Have you ever wondered what we would be like without a skeleton?
Just look at a jellyfish on the beach.

Jellyfish in the sea

A jellyfish uses the sea water to support its body. It doesn't have a skeleton.
So when it isn't in the sea, the jellyfish collapses.

Lose weight!

Space does funny things to people! When astronauts go into space they don't experience any gravity. Their bones don't have to support their weight. So their bones start to get thinner and lighter. Astronauts weigh less when they come back to Earth.

Go to bed early, grow very tall ... !

"Go to bed early, grow very tall, go to bed late, stay very small", or so they say!

When you go to bed, your backbone relaxes. The spongy discs in between the bones of your back relax as they are less squashed. So when you get up in the morning, you are very slightly taller than when you went to bed! Try measuring yourself. Is it true?

Things to do

How strong?

Bones are very strong. But they are also hollow. This is the best shape for bones so that they are strong but light enough to move.

- Roll sheets of paper to create different shaped towers. Place some books or weights on the top of the towers. Which one holds the most? How strong are hollow shapes?

Totally spineless

Worms, snails and slugs don't have a skeleton inside their body. How do they keep their shape?

- Look at a crab, or large insect. They have a skeleton on the outside of their body. How do you think they support themselves?

Exploring

Humans and other animals
Bones

Find out:

- more about your skeleton.
- what three jobs a skeleton does.

Did you know?

- We have tiny bones at the end of our backbones that were once tails! We also have some muscles, which most people can't work, that should wiggle our ears!
- The garfish has green bones!
- A snake can digest bones and teeth.

I wonder ...

If you put a tooth in cola or vinegar it will decay. What do you think might happen to a bone in cola or vinegar? Explain why.

Contracting muscles

Things to learn

- Our skeletons have muscles attached to them.
- Muscles contract to make bones move.
- Muscles work in pairs.

A nose like an elephant's

An elephant has a strong flexible nose. It has over 40 000 muscles in it! All these muscles mean the elephant can pick up a delicate flower or lift a huge log. The trunk can also touch, grasp, suck, spray, smell and strike!

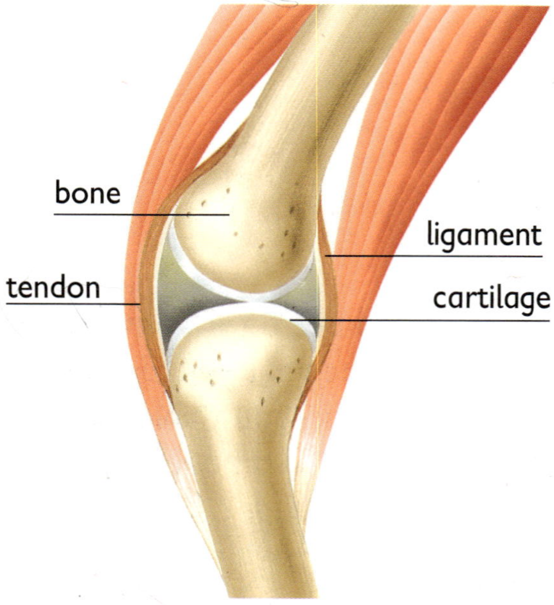

This is a hinge joint, which you find in your elbows, knees, fingers and toes

Our own motors and machines

If you think of the skeleton as giving protection and support, then the muscles are the motors of the body. Muscles are connected to our bones at the joints by **tendons**. A joint is where two bones meet, like your elbow or shoulder.

When the muscle **contracts** it pulls on the tendon, which pulls on the bone, to make it move. Muscles can pull (contract). They cannot push, only **relax**. We need two muscles at each joint, one to pull in one direction and the other to pull in the opposite direction. As one pulls, the other relaxes. They work in pairs.

Things to do

Contract and relax?

When you move your forearm up and down at the elbow, two sets of muscles are working.

- Place your hand on your upper arm. Can you feel which muscles contract when you lift your forearm? What happens to the muscles under your arm? Where are there other pairs of muscles in your body?

Caterpillars

- Watch a caterpillar moving across some paper. It has over 2000 muscles in its body. We have only 600. Does the caterpillar have a skeleton? Describe how the caterpillar moves. How do the muscles contract and relax?

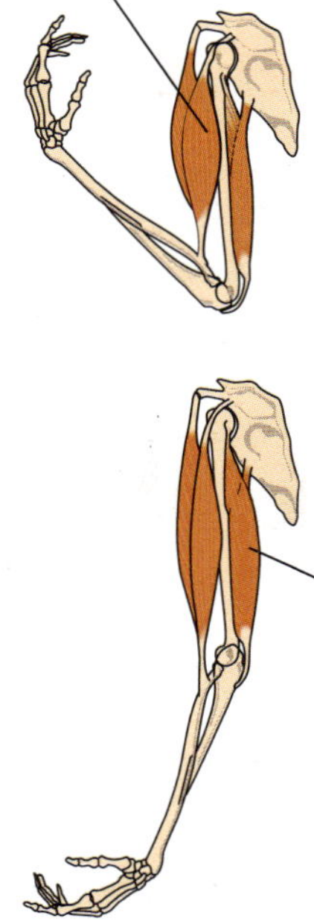

This a diagram of your arm, showing the biceps and triceps muscles

Digging deeper

Moving The muscles

Find out:

- more about muscles.
- the names of all the types of muscles.

Did you know?

- You need 72 muscles to speak a single word!
- It takes 17 facial muscles to smile, but 42 to frown, so smiling is easier!
- The layer of hairs on your body helps trap heat. Each hair is attached to a tiny muscle that makes the hair stand on end when you are cold! We call this muscle contraction 'goose pimples'.

I wonder ...

Watch someone smile and frown. Can you see the muscles contract?

Exercising muscles

Things to learn

- Muscles work harder when we exercise.
- We feel tired when muscles work hard.

Tireless muscle

Our muscles work everytime we move. Do you think all of them work at the same time? Your heart works all the time, even if you don't tell it to! It beats about 100 000 times each day. If you had to tell it to work, your heart would stop when you went to sleep. What would happen then?

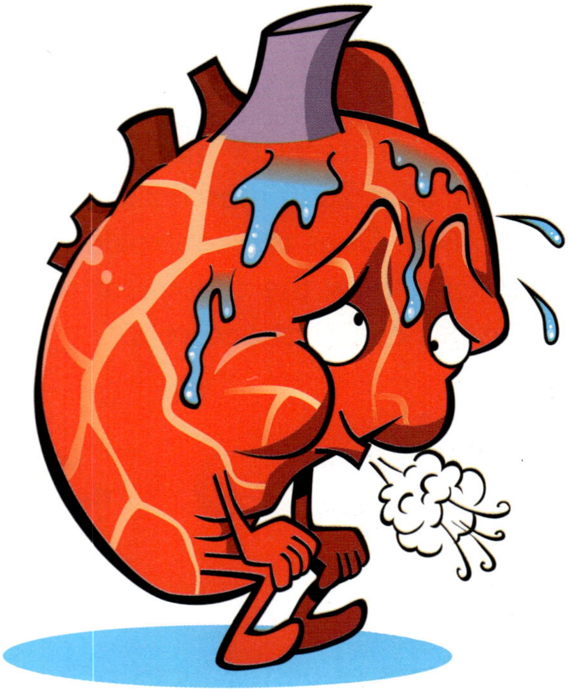

Your intestines pass the food along inside your body. They also work all the time. Do you have to tell them to work? Many parts of your body work without you thinking. Which muscles work when you think about them?

Muscles can grow

Have you ever watched competitions to find the strongest man or woman? These people have much bigger muscles than us. How do they grow them? Do you think it was easy to develop these muscles?

Try the activity on the next page and discover what happens when you exercise. How does exercise make you fit?

Things to do

Exercise

- Sit very still. And quiet! Think about how you feel. Close your eyes and pay attention to your body. Now get up and walk around the room. After a couple of minutes, stop. How is your body different?
- Now stand behind your chair. Put your hands on the top of the chair and start bobbing up and down. Stop as soon as you feel different. Explain the changes to your body. Why might you need to breathe faster?

Exercise keeps you fit

Digging deeper

Moving
Hands and feet

Find out:

- about hands and feet.
- what is so special about our hands.

Did you know?

- A cat has over 30 muscles in each earflap. We have only 6!
- Walking requires the use of 200 muscles in the human body. Of these, it takes 40 muscles to lift the leg and move it forward.
- Your heart is a hollow muscle about the same size as your fist. It pumps 36 000 litres of blood 12 000 miles every day!

I wonder ...

If you exercise regularly, your muscles become less tired. Why do you think this is?

4A Review

What have you learned?

- Some animals have internal skeletons like humans.
- Bones are very strong, but they can break.
- Our skeletons grow bigger as we grow up.
- Our skeletons support and protect our bodies and help us to move.
- We have muscles that work in pairs to help us move.

Find out more about ...

Life Processes and Living Things

- how bones grow and develop in babies.
- how Eadweard Muybridge discovered how animals move.

Check-up

Class 4W were having a PE lesson. They were running on the spot and felt tired.

- Draw and label a diagram to show how their muscles and bones worked together when they ran.
- Explain why they felt tired after exercise.

The answer!

Do you remember the question about recovering after a broken bone?

If you break your leg, the doctor puts a plaster cast on it to keep it still and straight. The bone will mend straight if it is kept still. As you are not using the muscles of that leg, they become weak. The leg becomes thin. You need to do some gentle exercise to build the muscles back up again.

4B Habitats

What do you know?

- Plants and animals are living things.
- Animals need food to grow and be healthy.
- Plants need light, warmth, air and water to grow well.
- Plants grow towards the Sun.

Would a dolphin survive in a wood? What about in a pond? Would a large tree grow big and strong in a pond? Every living thing, plant or animal, has its own special place to live that suits it best. This 'home address' is called its habitat.

Skills check

Can you ...

- measure time, distance and temperature?
- make careful observations?
- explain what you found out using what you know about science?

Words to learn

adaptation
classification
condition
consumer
environment
food chain
key
habitat
nutrition
organism
producer
variation
wild

Let's find out ...

Some people are very protective of the countryside. When they travel through it, they take care not to destroy it. They plant wild flowers in their gardens and leave logs lying around. This can look very untidy. So why do they do these things?

Different habitats

Things to learn

- A habitat is a place where plants and animals live naturally.
- Different animals and plants live in different habitats.
- Plants and animals survive best in their own habitat.

Where should we live?

We find camels in the deserts. We also find humans! We find polar bears in the Arctic. We also find humans! In fact, humans can live almost anywhere in the world! Unlike most animals, we wear clothes and live in houses to help us survive.

Camels live in the desert'

Penguins live in the Antarctic

In the desert we wear long, flowing, light robes. We wear cloths to protect our heads from the Sun. We build large houses of stone to keep us cool.

In the Arctic we wear thick furs. We keep our heads and hands warm. We wear boots on our feet. We also build houses that keep us warm. Plants and animals can't do that.

Are you in the habit?

Where do you go when you leave school? You probably go home. It's a habit. It is a habit to return to your home or habitat.

A **habitat** is a place where an animal or plant lives. It is a place that provides food and shelter. A habitat is a place where living things produce offspring.

Things to do

How many habitats?

Walk around the playground.

- Can you recognize any different habitats? Look at how different they are. What differences are there? How many different habitats can you describe around the school?

Where do you live?

Do you know where a snail would live? What about a frog or a butterfly?

- Visit some of your habitats and see if you were right. Why do these plants and animals live there?

Exploring

Living things in the environment
What is a habitat?

Find out:

- more about what a habitat is.
- if a camel could survive where a dolphin lives. Why not?

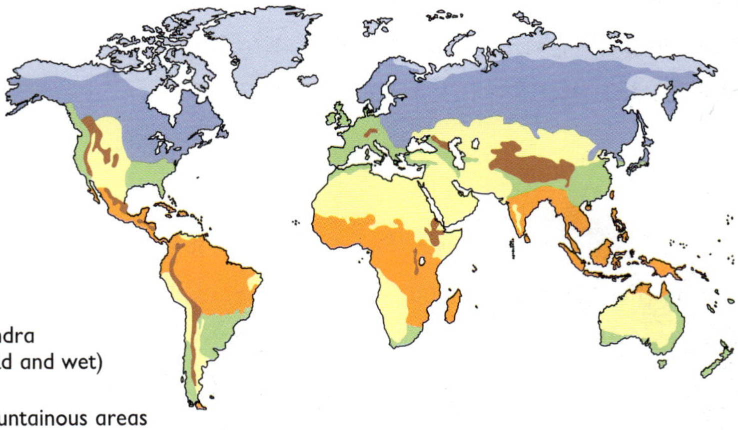

- Temperate (warm and wet)
- Tropical (hot and wet)
- Tundra (cold and wet)
- Polar (very cold and dry)
- Desert (dry)
- Mountainous areas where alttitude affects climate type

Did you know?

- The oceans are up to seven miles deep and cover over 70% of the world. The deep-sea habitat contains animals adapted to living in the dark.
- Camels have three eyelids to protect their eyes from blowing sand. They are adapted to life in the desert.

I wonder ...

It's cool, very wet and has lots of lilies and some animals. Lots of animals will die if they try to live in this habitat. Can you guess what the habitat is? What animals would you expect to find here?

Grouping living things

Things to learn

- There are similarities and differences between animals.
- Animals can be grouped by their similarities.
- Plants can also be grouped by their similarities.

Slugs and snails ...

"... and puppy dog tails. That's what little boys are made of." At least that's what they say! But why put slugs and snails with puppy dog tails? How are they alike? What else would you put with slugs and snails?

The same but different

All animals are alive. We all take in oxygen, feed, grow, reproduce, and move. But are all animals the same? Is a cat like a fish? Or a frog like a bird? Scientists have sorted all animals into groups. We are in a group called **mammals**. Mammals have a backbone, are warm-blooded, have fur or hair, have live babies and feed them with milk. Dogs, cats, whales and bats are also mammals. This means we are all in the same group. Are we like them? Could you put mammals into a smaller group?

Even a skunk is a mammal!

Plants are also sorted into groups. Some of them are trees, some are shrubs and some are grasses.

Things to do

What are you like?

Over 250 years ago a scientist called Carolus Linnaeus sorted living things into groups. This is called **classification**.

- Can you sort your own selection of plants and animals into groups? Try to explain how you have grouped them and why you put them into these groups. Some reasons for groups could be colour, shape, wings or number of legs. Can you think of some more?

Carolus Linnaeus devised the groups of plants and animals we use today

Exploring

Variation and classification
How living things are classified

Find out:

- more about how living things are classified.
- what language is used for the scientific names of plants and animals.

Did you know?

- Nearly one quarter of all mammals are bats!
- One large group of animals contains dogs, bears and cats – including big cats like the lion. Dogs, foxes and wolves all belong to the same, smaller group.
- When people first saw a giraffe, they called it a 'cameleopard'. They thought it came from a camel and a leopard!

Using keys

Things to learn

- Animals and plants can be identified by their features.
- We can identify them with keys.

Unlocking

Keys unlock things – they let you enter where you want to go. You use a key to get into your house. You even use a key, in the form of a password, on your computer. A key is also used to identify different and plants. It allows us to 'unlock' their identity.

What's my name?

Use Key 1 and Key 2 to find out the name of the man in this photo. Which key is easiest to use? Why?

Key 1

Q1	I am a man	Go to Q2
	I am a woman	Go to Q4
Q2	I have a beard	Go to Q3
	I do not have a beard	Go to Q5
Q3	My beard is grey	I am Louis Pasteur
	My beard is black	I am Wilhelm Rontgen
Q4	I have long hair	I am Amy Johnson
	I have short hair	I am Amelia Earhart
Q5	I wear glasses	I am Alexander Fleming
	I do not wear glasses	I am Edward Jenner

Key 2

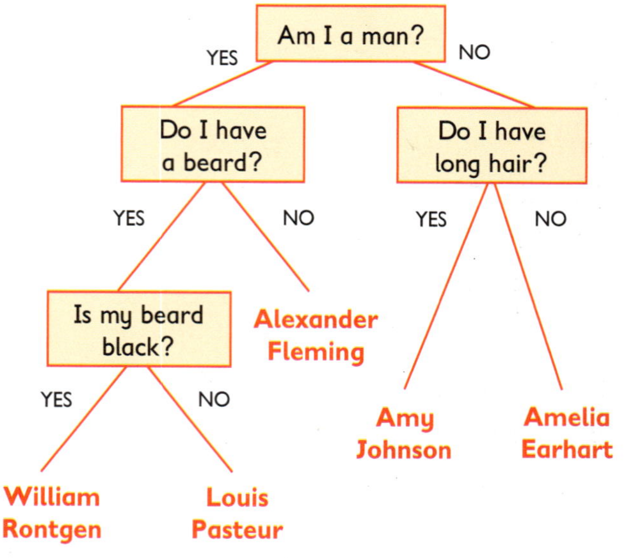

Things to do

What am I?

Can you identify a range of animals and plants? Go to one of your habitats and carefully collect some animals. Remember where you got them from, so you can return them later. Use some keys, like the ones on page 24, to identify them. Can you make your own key? Remember to ask simple questions that have 'yes' or 'no' answers. Try writing a key in both styles.

Biographies

Charles Darwin

Evolution is the process that has changed animals and plants over millions of years. It explains why plants and animals are found in different groups.

Find out:

- more about evolution and Charles Darwin.
- where he travelled to and what he found.

Did you know?

- Tomatoes are in the same group as the poisonous plant 'deadly nightshade'.
- The banana and a beautiful plant called 'the bird of paradise' are from the same family of plants!
- The giant kelps that make up underwater forests are in the same group as algae, which are usually tiny!

I wonder ...

Make up an animal. How would you name it so that everyone could identify it? Think carefully about how it looks. Use your description to give it a name.

Investigating woodlice

Your challenge

- Discover what **conditions** woodlice like to live in.
- Make a reliable observation.
- Explain your evidence scientifically.

What to do

The Cubs discussed all the conditions and habitats they thought that woodlice might like. They set up a fish tank with lots of different areas. They put woodlice in the tank. They agreed to leave the tank alone for a day to see what happened. The Cubs counted the woodlice before they put them in. They had 30 woodlice. Why did they do this? Would you use any of their ideas?

What you need

- a digital camera or a video camera with a timer
- a fish tank
- leaves, stones, twigs, soil, moss, compost, bark, sand

What to check

Now try it yourselves.

- What information are you going to collect?
- What do you think will happen?

What did you find?

The Cubs drew a table of their results after a day.

Habitat in tank	Number of woodlice
leaves	5
wet soil	2
dry soil	0
bark	5
stones	1
twigs	3

- Draw a table of your results or use the Cubs' results. Use a computer to record your results and draw a chart. What kind of chart or graph do you think would be best?
- What does your chart show? Which habitat did the woodlice like best?

Can you do better?

What would you do differently if you tried this again? Would using more woodlice improve the experiment? What about different habitats?

Now predict

- The Brownies are going out to collect woodlice so they can draw them. Where would you tell them to look for woodlice?
- The Beavers don't want to collect woodlice. They have decided to look for centipedes. Where do you think you would find a centipede? Why?
- Why was it better to use lots of woodlice rather than just a few?

Food chains

Things to learn

- Some animals eat other animals in their habitat.
- A food chain shows who eats who, or what, in a habitat.

Where does it come from?

All animals eat to give them energy. The energy is needed to grow and be active. But where does that energy come from? If you were a fox, you would get your energy by eating a rabbit. The rabbit got its energy from grass. The grass got its energy from the Sun. This description can be shown as a simple flow chart called a **food chain**. The arrows show what eats what.

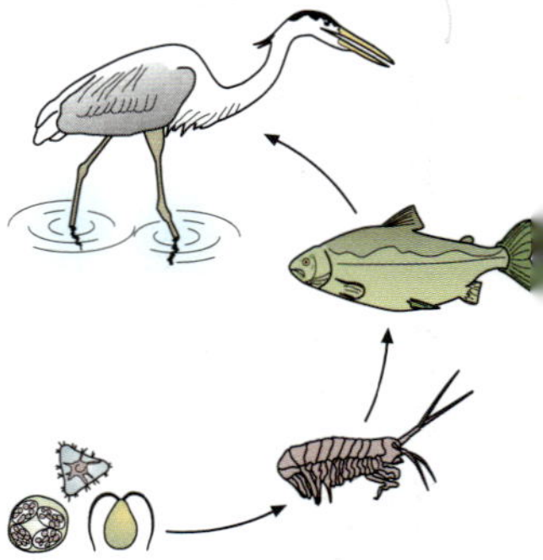

A freshwater food chain

Predator and prey

An animal that eats another animal is called a **predator**. The animal it eats is called its **prey**. Can you spot the predators and prey in these food chains? A predator may also be the prey of another animal!

A green plant is called a producer because it produces the food for other animals. How does the Sun help it to produce this food? Which are the producers in these food chains?

A woodland food chain

Things to do

Short and simple

- How can you turn a list of what an animal eats into a food chain? The arrows show the direction that the energy is flowing, that is, from the Sun to the animal.
- Look at some of the habitats around your school and produce a food chain for each one. You will need to observe what each organism eats. What does each food chain start with?
- Produce a food chain for an animal you might find in the zoo, like a bear or a snake.

This brown bear looks hungry ...

Digging deeper

Food chains
How food chains work

Find out:

- more about how food chains work.
- what a food web is.

Did you know?

- A shark is an efficient predator. It can smell blood when there is only one drop in 100 million gallons of sea water! It can also smell it from over ten miles away.
- The blue whale is the largest animal on Earth, but it lives on some of the smallest animals – krill and small shrimp-like crustaceans.
- A humpback whale eats 5000 fish a day. The fish will have eaten 7000 shrimps. The shrimps will have eaten 130 000 tiny green plants. So, it takes four billion green plants to feed a humpback whale every day!

I wonder ...
Where does all energy originally come from? Where do the plants get their energy from?

Changing habitats

Things to learn

- Animals are **adapted** to their habitat.
- Living things and their habitats need protecting.

All change

Could you imagine your cat living on the plains of Africa, catching and killing buffalo? What about keeping a tiger in your sitting room? Not very practical is it! But they are both cats. How are they different?

Each of them has adapted to suit where they live. The tiger has large claws and jaws for catching its prey. Our house cats have smaller claws and jaws.

The tiger is a member of the cat family

Do you want to visit my place?

The rabbit isn't adapted to living in the pond. Can you explain why? What animals *are* adapted to living in the pond? The fish isn't adapted to living in the rabbit's habitat? Why do you think this is? Can you think of other animals that are adapted to the rabbit's habitat?

Some animals can live in two different habitats. A frog is adapted to live in the habitats of both the rabbit and the fish. Can you explain why? Can you name some other animals that are adapted to living in two different habitats?

Things to do

Save our habitat

- Walk around your school playground. Look at the habitats. Have they changed since you first looked at them? What do you think would happen if someone started to build a house on the playing field? Or filled in the pond? Think about the animals and the plants that live there.
- Not all fungi are safe to eat. But imagine you have found a new mushroom, a fungus that you can safely eat. It lives on damp ground with lots of shade. Then someone cuts down all the trees. Write a letter to your local councillor and ask him to save the habitat of your mushroom. Explain why it is important to keep the trees.

Exploring

Living things in their environment
Protecting the environment

Find out:

- more about protecting the **environment**.
- what else we need to protect the environment from.

Did you know?

- To save a 12 metre high tree, a 1·2 metre stack of newspapers would have to be recycled.
- A plastic container could take as long as 50 000 years to rot away!

I wonder ...

What can you do to protect the environment in your area?

4B Review

What have you learned?

- Different animals and plants are found in different habitats.
- Plants and animals can be grouped by features they have in common.
- To create and use a key to identify some animals and plants.
- Animals and plants are adapted to their environment.
- We need to protect the habitats that animals and plants live in.

Find out more about ...

Life Processes and Living Things

- how some animals are changed to suit their environment.
- how changing the habitat affects the animals and plants living there.

Check-up

The youth group are going on a nature walk. They need to treat their environment carefully so that they don't disturb the animals and plants living there.

- Explain why they should not damage habitats.
- Explain why they mustn't break any food chains.
- Explain why there will be more plants and animals if we care for more habitats.

Even this old oak tree with a rotten centre provides food and shelter for many plants and animals

The answer!

Remember the first question? Wild flowers provide bees and other insects with a source of food. Logs provide places for small animals like woodlice and beetles to live. Not being too tidy in the garden helps wildlife to survive. It gives them shelter and food. It provides their habitat – their home address.

4C Keeping warm

What do you know?

- Materials have many different properties.
- Some materials have similar properties.
- Some properties are more useful to us than others.
- Some materials are good electrical conductors and some are good electrical insulators.

If you go to the beach in summer, what do you wear? How does the sea feel after you've been playing in the Sun? Do you want hot soup or ice cream for lunch? What will happen to the ice cream if you don't eat it fast enough? Would the same happen on a cold day?

Skills check

Can you …

- read a ruler accurately?
- use a computer for your work?

Words to learn

Celsius
conduct
degrees
electricity
heat
insulate
insulation
temperature
thermal
thermometer

Let's find out …

Heat rises, which means that the top of your home can be hotter than the bottom. If you live in a house, the loft is the hottest place. In winter you want to keep that heat. A layer of material is put in the loft to help keep the heat in. We call this layer **insulation**. What material would slow down the escape of heat? Will insulation make the house warmer if there is no heating?

Feeling hot

Things to learn

- **Temperature** is a measure of how hot or cold things are.
- A **thermometer** measures temperature.
- Our senses are not accurate thermometers.

Which sense do you use to tell the flame is hot?

Sense of ...

How many senses do you have? Where are they found in your body? You have five senses – touch, taste, sight, hearing and smell. They are all found on your head. The sense of touch is also found all over your body. What do you use for sensing heat? Can you smell heat or see it? Can you hear it?

What temperature should the thermometer read if the child is well?

Feeling hot

When you are ill, an adult may touch your forehead. They may say you 'have a temperature'. They mean that you are warmer than usual. A high temperature may mean you are not well. But touching your forehead does not give an accurate temperature. A thermometer can measure how hot you are. Normally your body temperature should be 37° C. This means that on a thermometer with a **Celsius** scale, your temperature reads 37. Some thermometers have a Fahrenheit (F) scale. Your temperature should be 98·4° F.

Things to do

Heat sense

How do you know if something is 'hot'? If it is safe, you may feel it. You use your sense of touch. Is this good enough?

- Put both your hands into a bowl of hot tap water. Then place one hand in a bowl of cold water, and the other in a bowl of warm water. How would you describe what you felt to another person?

Exploring

Changing materials
Measuring temperature

Find out:

- about different kinds of thermometer.
- if medical thermometers that change colour with temperature are accurate.

I wonder ...

Thermometers are filled with alcohol and a dye, so they look red, green or blue. Some older thermometers are filled with mercury. Why is this no longer used?

Did you know?

- The first medical thermometer was made by Thomas Allbutt in 1867.
- Theodore Hannes Benzinger, a surgeon in World War II, invented the ear thermometer, to take human body temperature.
- Thermometers work because the liquid in them expands or contracts until it is the same temperature as the surroundings. This can be measured on a temperature scale.

Measuring temperature

Things to learn

- A thermometer measures temperature.
- There are lots of different thermometers.
- Thermometers must be handled with care.
- Objects gain or lose heat until they reach room temperature.

How hot?

A thermometer is used to measure how hot or cold something is. This is called 'taking a temperature'. A thermometer has a liquid in it that expands (gets bigger) when the object gets hotter. This shows the temperature rising. If the liquid in the thermometer is high, the object is hot.

Work out what temperatures these thermometers are showing. Which is the hottest temperature?

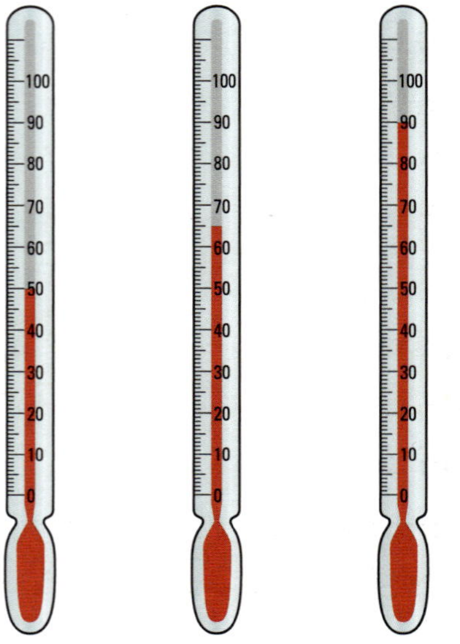

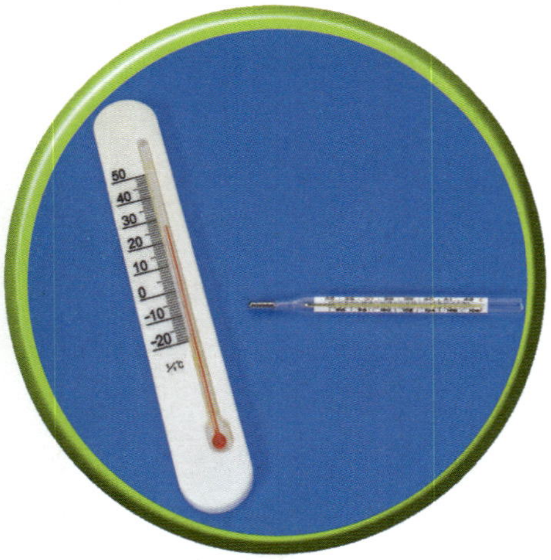

Different objects are used to record temperatures in different places. Some are used outside, some in science and some for people. Where do you think we would use these thermometers?

Goldilocks

Remember the story of *Goldilocks and the Three Bears*? Why did the bears go for a walk? What happened to the porridge after it was made? The bowls of porridge lost their heat to the air, until the porridge was the same temperature as the air around it – room temperature. The opposite happens with cold things. They gain heat from the air, until they are the same temperature as the air – and the room.

Things to do

Final temperature

What temperature is your classroom? Use a thermometer to find out.

- Place five marked beakers in a row. Half fill each one with water from different places, like the fridge, or the hot or cold tap. Take the starting temperature of the water in each beaker. Write it down. Then take it again an hour later.
- Use the thermometer properly. Keep the bulb of the thermometer in the water. Bend down so that your eye is level with the thermometer. Keep the thermometer upright. Don't stir the liquid with the thermometer. What will happen if you leave the water and take its temperature after one day? What has happened? Why? What pattern or rule is there about temperatures over time?

Biographies

Biographies
Gabriel Daniel Farenheit

Find out:

- more about the first modern thermometer made by Gabriel Daniel Fahrenheit.
- what Fahrenheit used to fill his thermometers.

Did you know?

- America is the only country still using the Fahrenheit scale for measuring temperature. All other countries use the Celsius scale.
- There are several different scales for measuring temperature, including Fahrenheit, Kelvin, Celsius, Reaumur and Rankine!

I wonder ...

If you put beakers of water at different temperatures in a fridge, what final temperature would they all have?

Hot and cold places

Things to learn

- Different places are at different temperatures.
- 20° C is a comfortable room temperature.

Bring me sunshine!

What is the temperature like when you go on holiday? Does it depend on where you go? If you listen to weather reports, they tell you the temperature for the next day. What pattern do you notice about the temperatures? If you wanted to be warm, where on this map would you go?

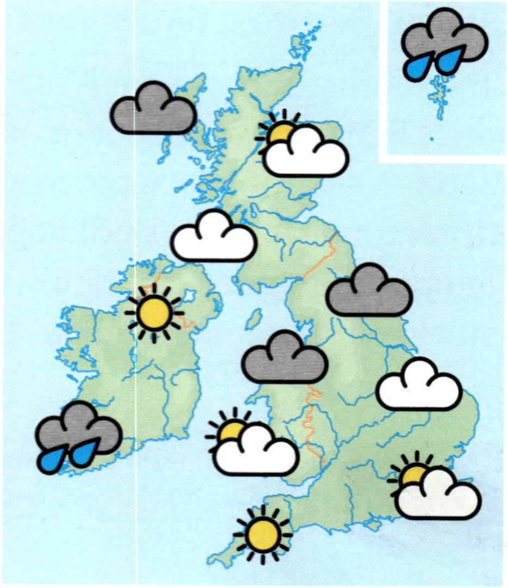

Keeping your cool

Look at this 'map' of a kitchen. Where would you put some seedlings to grow well? Where would you keep your can of fizzy drink so that it didn't fizz over when you opened it? Would this be a hot or a cold place? What helped you to decide?

Are all the places in this kitchen the same temperature? If you had an ice lolly where would you keep it? What would happen if you didn't?

Things to do

Hot spots

- Draw a 'map' of your classroom. If you were cold, where would you want to sit? Why? If you were too hot you might want to sit in a different place. Is there any scientific reason for this?
- Put a blue cross on your 'map' where you think it will be cool. Put a red cross where you think it is warmer. How could you discover if you are right?
- Plan your investigation carefully. Choose the place and the type of thermometer. Mark red and blue circles to show your results on your map.
- Why is it warmer in some places than in others?

Exploring

Grouping and classifying materials
Conducting heat

Find out:

- which materials conduct heat. We call these 'good thermal conductors'.
- what a 'poor thermal conductor' is called.

The plastic cool box is a poor thermal conductor. It doesn't allow heat to travel inside.

Did you know?

- We have heating in our homes to keep the temperature inside stable. 20° C is a comfortable room temperature.
- Air-conditioning units keep buildings around this temperature in the summer.

I wonder ...

Will another classroom be at a different temperature? Where will the hot and cool spots be? Why?

Keeping cool

Your challenge

- Use a thermometer carefully and accurately.
- Discover the best way to keep ice lollies cold.
- Explain what you found out.

What to do

Kavita has got ice lollies for her friends. It's a sunny day, and she has to get the ice lollies to her friends before they **melt**. Will insulation keep the lollies cold and solid? What would you do?

What you need

- a thermometer
- a stopwatch
- ice lollies
- pieces of different fabrics

What to check

Now try it yourselves.

- What will you use to keep the ice lollies cold?
- Does the starting size of each ice lolly matter?
- How will you measure how well the lollies survive the journey?
- How will you measure whether your ice lolly has stayed cold?

What did you find?

Kavita measured how long her lollies were when she took them to her friends. These are her results.

Method of insulation	Length of lolly (cm)
in socks	12
in hat	13
in cardboard	14
in pocket	11

- Draw a graph of Kavita's results.
- Which method of insulation kept the lollies from melting most? How can you tell?
- What was happening to the lollies?
- Draw a graph of your own results. What sort of graph can you draw? Try using a computer to draw your graph as well.
- Which of your insulation methods kept the ice lollies coldest?

Can you do better?

Kavita measured the length of her lollies to see which melted the most. What other measurement could she have taken?

Did you use a thermometer? How often did you take the temperature of the ice lollies?

Now predict

- If you wrapped different ice lollies in different thicknesses of newspaper sheets, how long would the lollies stay frozen?
- What is the newspaper doing?

Investigating insulators

DO NOT use boiling water

Your challenge

- Discover how to keep liquid hot for a long time.
- Decide what an insulator does.
- Explain what you found out.

What to do

The Hiking Club are going for a walk. They are taking hot soup with them.

Harry has put his soup in a thermos flask.

A thermos flask insulates things – heat can't get in or out easily.

What would you use? Try with hot water from a tap. You must be fair. Change the material of the container or the fabric it is wrapped in. What must you keep the same?

Here are some of the ideas the oth hikers had to keep their soup warm

a plastic cup with a lid

a metal container with a lid

a plastic cup with a lid, wrapped in a jumper

a metal container with a lid, wrapped in a jumper

a plastic cup with a lid, wrapped in a hankie

a metal container with a lid, wrapped in a hankie

What you need

- mugs or containers with lids
- small items of clothing
- thermometers
- a stopwatch
- a measuring jug
- warm tap water

What to check

Now try it yourselves.

- Are all your starting temperatures the same?
- Are you keeping all your containers in the same place?

What did you find?

These are the hikers' results:

Container and insulation	Temperature after 40 minutes (°C)
plastic cup with lid	65
metal container with lid	55
plastic cup with lid in a jumper	75
metal container with lid in a jumper	64
plastic cup with lid in a cotton hanky	67
metal container with lid in a cotton hanky	59

- Draw a graph of the hikers' results. What type of graph will you draw? Draw one using a computer as well. Which were the best ways of keeping their soup warm?
- From what you found out, which fabric is best at insulating? Look at the fabric carefully. Use a hand lens. What makes a good thermal insulator?

Can you do better?

The hikers tested what they would normally carry in their backpacks. What else could you test?

Was the hikers' test fair? Why?

Now predict

- Does it matter what the starting temperature of the soup is?
- Air is a good thermal insulator. Trapped air in a woollen jumper is warmed by the soup. So the soup is wrapped in a warm 'air overcoat'.

Conducting heat

Things to learn

- Metals are not good insulators.
- Good electrical conductors are often good **thermal** conductors too.
- Thermal insulators are useful.

Hot or cold?

Any material that slows the movement of heat is an insulator. If the heat can't get in, it can't get out either. An insulator keeps hot things hot and cold things cold. The same materials will insulate both hot and cold objects. But not both at once!

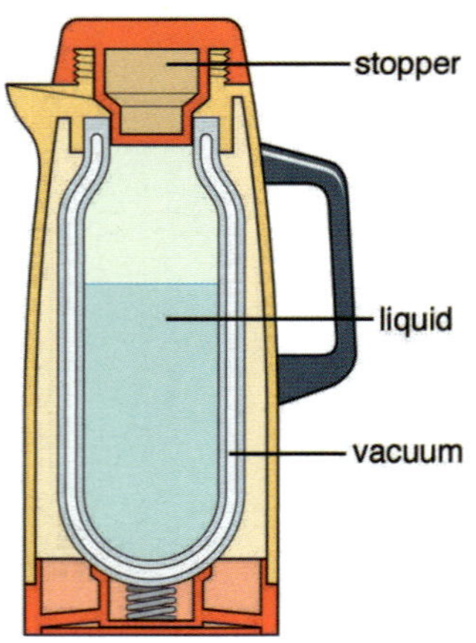

Vacuum flasks

A vacuum flask is a good insulator. It is like one jug inside another. Between the two jugs there is nothing at all – a vacuum. Heat cannot travel easily through air – but it cannot travel at all through a vacuum. Hot food in a vacuum flask stays hot. Cold food stays cold. The food still loses heat through the stopper but very slowly!

Thermal underwear

Thermal means heat. What does thermal underwear do? It keeps you warm. It stops the heat from your body escaping into the air. In winter you would put on more layers of clothes. The thick fabrics trap air. You warm the air, and so you keep warm. But clothes aren't hot themselves. They are at room temperature.

These clothes trap lots of air to keep your heat in

Things to do

Runny honey

Find out which materials are good thermal conductors. This means that they **conduct** heat easily.

- Collect spoons of different materials. Put a small amount of thick honey on the end of each handle. Put the spoons in bowls of hot water and start your stopwatch. Record how long it takes for the honey to go runny on each spoon. On which spoon did the honey melt fastest? Which material conducted the heat fastest?
- Which material would you use to make a saucepan? Which material would you use for the handle?

This saucepan is made of only one material. Why might the handle get hot?

Digging deeper

Changing materials
Temperature changes

Find out:

- more about temperature and heat travelling.
- which way heat travels.

Did you know?

- Polar bears have two layers of fur. This traps air close to their body and keeps their body heat in. They have a thick layer of fat under their skin, which is a good insulator.

I wonder ...

Metals are good thermal conductors. They are also good conductors of electricity. Are good thermal insulators good electrical insulators too?

4C Review

Never handle loft insulation material without wearing gloves.

What have you learned?

- Temperature is a measure of how hot or cold things are.
- A thermometer measures temperature accurately.
- There are different kinds of thermometers.
- Objects gain or lose heat until they reach room temperature.
- Thermal conductors allow heat to travel through them easily and fast.
- Thermal insulators slow the movement of heat.
- Air is a good thermal insulator; thick fabrics trap air.
- Metals are poor insulators.
- Good electrical conductors are often good thermal conductors too.
- How to use a thermometer carefully and accurately.
- You must handle a thermometer with care.

Find out more about ...

Materials and their Properties

- wool and why it is used for clothes.
- molecules cooling down.

Check-up

It's very cold outside and Mr Simpson wants to make sure he stays warm and cosy. He has the heating turned right up, but this costs a lot of money.

What else could Mr Simpson do to keep himself warm?

The answer!

Remember the first question? Loft insulation is very thick with loose fibres. It looks like yellow cotton wool. It has air trapped in it. The trapped air helps to insulate the house. The heat that has risen to the loft can't easily escape from the house. This makes it warmer indoors!

If the house isn't warm, then there isn't any heat to keep in. Loft insulation only keeps in the heat that is already there.

4D Separating solids and liquids

What do you know?

- Some materials are natural and some are made.
- Materials have different properties.
- Heating and cooling can cause some materials to change.
- What happens to water when it is heated and cooled.
- How to use a sieve to separate different-sized solid particles.

Everything in the world is made up of 'matter' – the scientific word for 'stuff'. The air all around us is matter, even though we can't see it! There are three types of matter – **solids**, **liquids** and **gases**. These are called the 'states' of matter. Sometimes matter can be changed from one 'state' to another. You are going to learn about two of the states, liquids and solids, and how they can be separated. Gases come later!

Skills check

Can you …

- make careful observations and measurements?
- collect evidence and see how good it is?
- use your evidence to explain what you've found out?
- use your evidence to predict something you don't yet know?

Words to learn

dissolve
dissolved
filter
freeze
insoluble
liquid
melt
particle
separate
sieve
solid
solidify
soluble
solution
undissolved

Let's find out …

The river near Jane's school is polluted. The Scouts and the Guides have cleared away all the rubbish they could find from the river and its banks. The water looks very clean and clear but fish still won't live in it. What can the problem be?

Properties of materials

Things to learn

- Materials are made up of **particles**.
- Materials can exist as solids, liquids or gases.
- The particles in solids, liquids and gases are arranged in different ways.
- Heating and cooling materials can change their properties.

Atomic Greek

About 2500 years ago, a Greek scientist thought that if you kept cutting a material in half, it would eventually be too small to divide any more. He called this smallest possible particle an 'atom'. It would take millions of atoms to cover the full stop at the end of this sentence. Now that's small! All matter is made up of atoms. Different arrangements of atoms or particles make different materials. A material is either a solid or a liquid depending upon how its particles are arranged. If the particles move freely then it is a gas.

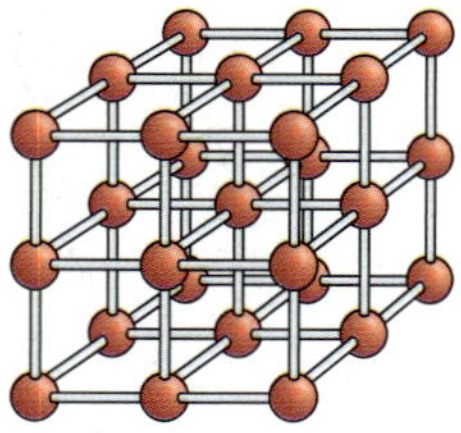

Shape up

Imagine how closely together fruit is packed in boxes. This is how particles in a solid are packed. Solids, like a book or block of wood, have a structure and a shape that's not easy to change. Even tiny pieces of solid – like sugar – have their own shape.

Get moving

Have you played in a ball pond? The balls are like particles in a liquid. They are still quite close together but they can move around each other. This lets a liquid flow.

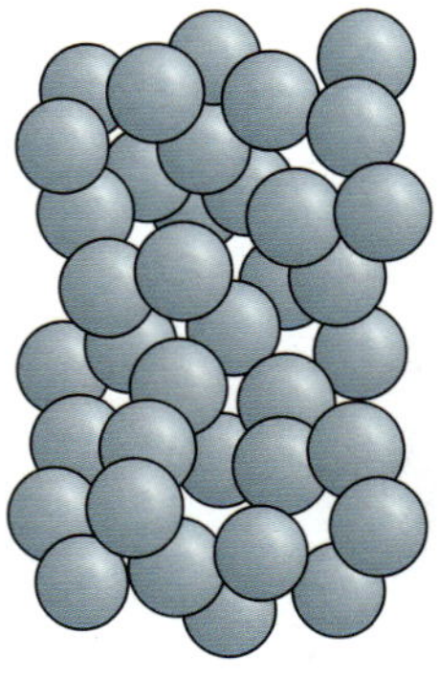

All change

Solids can melt and become liquid when they are heated. Liquids can become solid if they are cooled down enough. Melting and freezing can be reversed.

Things to do

Measure water

Look at some water in a glass. You can see that the water doesn't have its own shape. It takes the shape of the glass. When water is poured into different containers, its volume (how much of it there is) stays the same but its shape changes.

- Find some different-shaped containers. Fill them with water and see what shape the water takes.
- Look at the top of the water. You'll see that it's level. Try tipping it. What happens to the water level now? Liquids always have a flat top!

Digging deeper

Materials and their properties
Solids, liquids and gases Using liquids

Find out:

- how engineers use liquids as lubrication, fuel and to make things move in hydraulic machines.
- how the properties of liquids are useful to us.

Did you know?

- Long ago, scientists called alchemists tried to make gold from other materials. But it's impossible!
- Most metals are solid but mercury is liquid at room temperature.
- The temperature on Neptune is so low that no liquids can exist.

I wonder ...

What solid water looks like. Maybe you know!

Solids and liquids

Your challenge

- Identify solids, liquids and solids that act like liquids.

The crew of the Starship Venture need to find a cure for a deadly virus on planet Xerex. But Captain Berzelius has a problem. All of the labels on his first aid kit have been removed ...

What to do

How could the Captain recognize the correct medicine? How could the Doctor describe it to him?

Look carefully at a collection of materials. Think how you could group them.

Could you pour your material? Is it a solid or a liquid? What happens when you mix it with water? What does it smell like?

Remember, the crew can't taste their materials. They could be dangerous!

What you need

- a selection of materials
- a hand lens or magnifying glass
- a beaker
- water
- a spoon
- a measuring cylinder

What to check

Now try it yourselves.

- What tests will you do to decide which materials are solid, and which liquid?
- What about the materials that are like both?
- Will you keep the quantities of your materials the same?

What did you find?

The Doctor gave Captain Berzelius a set of instructions to sort out the materials. First, he needed to sort out the liquids from the solids. He needed to do several tests. Here is his first set of results.

Mystery material	Has its own shape (or can be piled up)?	Forms drips when poured?	Keeps a level surface when tipped?	Liquid or solid?
1 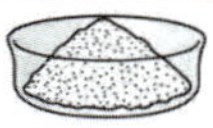	yes	no	no	solid
2 	no	yes	yes	liquid
3 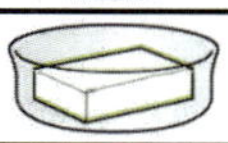	yes	can't be poured	no	solid
4 	no	yes	yes	liquid
5 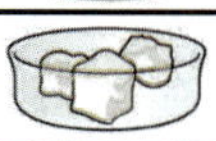	yes	can't be poured	no	solid
6 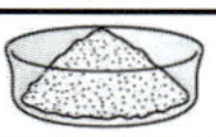	yes	no	no	solid
7 	no	yes	yes	liquid
8 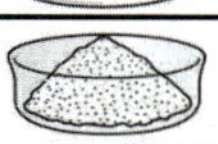	yes	no	no	solid
9 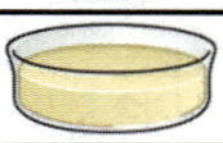	no	yes	yes	liquid
10 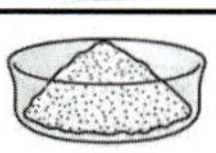	yes	no	no	solid

- Captain Berzelius sorted out which materials were solid and which were liquid. Was he right?
- What happens to the liquids if we change the containers they're in?
- What other tests separate liquids from solids?

Can you do better?

How good is your evidence? Can you make a general rule about your results?

Can you make a key to identify your materials?

Now predict

The Captain discovered that some solids could behave like liquids if they had tiny particles.

- How would you group jelly, custard, toothpaste, tomato ketchup, whipped cream and hair gel? Are they solids, liquids or something else?

Changing materials

Your challenge

- Find out how materials can be changed by heating and cooling.
- Discover if some changes can be reversed.

What would happen to the ice cream if it were left on the table for a long time? Why did Mum want to put the chocolate biscuits back into the fridge?

What to do

After her party Rosie decided to find out more about how things change from solids to liquids and back again. She put small pieces of food in cake cases and floated them on hot water.

What you need

- butter, margarine, solid vegetable fat, milk chocolate, dark chocolate, jelly cube, ice cube
- a bowl
- hot tap water
- cake cases
- small paper flags

What to check

Now try it yourselves.

- What are you going to measure?
- How will you decide if something has melted?
- How are you going to check and record your results?

What did you find?

Rosie chose some foods to test. As the foods heated on the hot water, she wrote down what she saw:

Test material	What happened when it was heated
butter	melted quickly
margarine	melted slowly
vegetable fat	melted quickly
milk chocolate	melted quickly
dark chocolate	melted slowly
jelly cube	melted really slowly
ice cube	melted fastest

Rosie left the foods to cool. She noticed that the butter, margarine, chocolate and fat became solid again but the ice cube was still liquid. She put it in the fridge but it still didn't **solidify**.

- What must she do to turn the water back into ice?

Can you do better?

How good is your evidence?

How many more foods can you find to test?

Now predict

Rosie's mum is baking a cake. She gets the margarine out of the fridge and heats it in the microwave oven for a few seconds. Why does she do that?

Separating materials

Things to learn

- Mixtures of solids can sometimes be separated.
- Mixtures of solids and liquids can sometimes be separated.
- The different properties of materials can help us to separate them.

All mixed up

When two or more materials are mixed together we get a mixture. Look at a packet of soup mix. It might contain dried pasta, beans, vegetables and spices. Some mixtures are harder to recognize. Mayonnaise is a mixture of oil and eggs but it just looks like one creamy substance. How many mixtures can you think of?

Sieve it

A **sieve** will hold back anything with particles bigger than the size of its holes. Different sieves have different sizes of holes. You can separate large (coarse) particles and small (fine) particles.

We can also use sieves to separate some solids from liquids. At home, you might have a special sieve called a 'colander'. This separates vegetables from the water they have been cooked in.

Paper sieves

Sometimes we need to separate very small solid particles that have been mixed with liquids. A normal sieve might not do the job. But we could try paper. Paper has very small holes and is like a mini-sieve. Liquids can pass through but tiny particles of solids are left behind. This is called **filtering**.

Look at a tea bag or a coffee filter paper with a hand lens. What can you see?

Things to do

Make a mixture

- Mix together different-sized dry solids. Try rice and salt, or lentils, sugar and pasta shapes. How many sieves will you need to separate them? Can you work out which sieve to use first?

Filter it out

Which materials make the best filters?

- Try a selection of different papers and cloths to filter some muddy water. Use a funnel to help you. Which do you think will work best? Look at your materials closely with a hand lens. Does that give you any clues? Which is the fastest and which the slowest?

Digging deeper

Separating materials
Sieves and filters

Find out:

- more about what filters are made from.
- how we use filters in cars and at home.

Did you know?

- The hairs in your nose form a filter. They stop dirt and dust getting into your lungs.
- Gunpowder is a mixture of a mineral, yellow sulphur, and charcoal. It was first discovered in China over 3000 years ago.
- A mixture of ice cream and air makes soft, creamy, whipped ice cream.

I wonder ...

Jake squeezes some oranges but he gets pips and bits of orange pulp in his juice. How can he separate them from the juice?

Heating and cooling

Things to learn

- The same material can exist at different temperatures.
- Heating a solid can make it change to a liquid.
- Cooling a liquid can make it change to a solid.
- Water exists in three states – solid, liquid and gas.
- Heating or cooling water changes its state.

Turn up the heat

Many materials can be both solids and liquids, depending on their temperature. Metal is usually solid. but becomes liquid if it is hot enough. The Earth's core is so hot that normally solid rocks melt. Liquid rock, called lava, can erupt from volcanoes.

Disappearing acts

When some solids are mixed with water they seem to disappear. But do they? Sugar **dissolves** in water perfectly. It spreads throughout the water to make a sugar **solution**. Could you use a filter to get the sugar back?

Water, water everywhere

We can find water on Earth in all three states, as water, ice and water vapour. Look what happens if you put water in the freezer.

The freezer is below 0°C. The water freezes into ice, but white spirit stays liquid.

The fridge is just above 0°C. The water melts back to water, but butter stays solid.

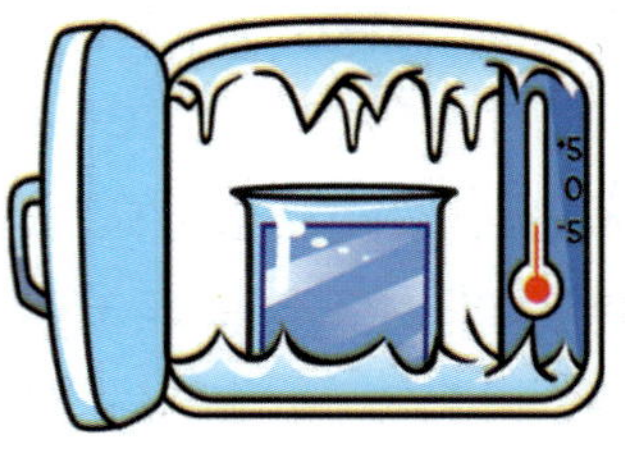

What do you think will happen if the water is put back into the freezer?

Things to do

Water marks

Bottled water has special mineral salts dissolved in it. These can make it very good to drink.

- Pour some different mineral waters onto some clear saucers. Try tap water too. Leave the water to dry up for a few days, then see what's left behind. You should see a fine powder. These are chemicals that have been dissolved in the water. Try looking at them through a microscope. Where has the water has gone?

Salt rings left after the water has evaporated

Kitchen chemistry

Not only solids dissolve in water; liquids do too. When you make a drink of orange squash, you're dissolving the squash in the water. Do all liquids dissolve in water?

- Try mixing some small amounts of oil, vinegar, milk, syrup, washing-up liquid or fruit juice. Draw what you see.

Digging deeper

Solids, liquids and gases
Melting and freezing

Find out:

- more about melting and freezing.
- what happens when you freeze salty water in the investigation 'Cooling down'.

Did you know?

- 98% of the world's water is liquid. Less than 2% of the water is ice.
- The Ice Hotel in Sweden is the world's biggest igloo. It is made completely from ice and is rebuilt every December.

I wonder ...

Ponds often freeze in winter but the sea rarely freezes. Why is that?

Dissolving solids

Your challenge

- Find out which solids dissolve in water and which don't.
- Find out how to get insoluble solids back.
- Find out how to get dissolved solids back.

On the Starship Venture, Captain Berzelius is trying to find medicine D51.

What to do

The Captain poured 100 ml of cold water into six beakers. Then he mixed a level teaspoon of each solid with the water. He stirred each mixture for exactly one minute. He let the mixture settle and looked at the result.

What do you think? Decide what to measure and how you'll record your results.

What you need

- a selection of safe white solids
- a measuring cylinder
- transparent beakers
- a teaspoon
- a funnel
- filter paper
- a magnifying glass or hand lens
- a seconds timer
- a petri dish or saucer

What to check

Now try it yourselves.

- What are you going to measure?
- How will you know when your substance has dissolved?
- How many times will you repeat the investigation? Why is this a good idea?
- How will you keep the test fair?

What did you find?

The Captain tested the six solids and made a table of his results:

Sample substance		Appearance after one minute when mixed with cold water
1	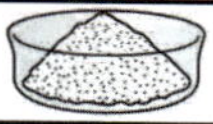	Turns water cloudy, white powder sinks to bottom of beaker.
2	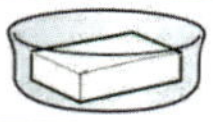	Some of the solid disappears but most stays in lumps.
3	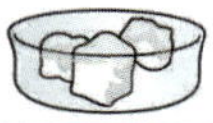	Solid sinks to bottom of beaker.
4	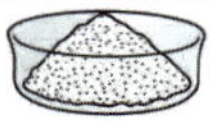	Some frothing, most of the solid remains undissolved.
5	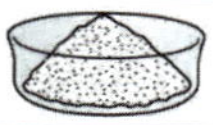	Solid disappears completely.
6	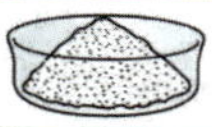	Solid dissolves but turns liquid white.

- Make a chart of your results. You could use a computer program to help you.

Can you do better?

How good is your evidence?
What would you do differently if you did this again?
Would the temperature of the water make a difference?

Now predict

- How can the Captain get the solids out of the water? Can he get them all back? What about the ones that have dissolved?
- Mix some sand and some salt in water. Think about how you could get both the salt and the sand back.

4D Review

What have you learned?

- Everything in the world is made of materials.
- Materials can be solid, liquid or a gas.
- Heating or cooling materials can make them change.
- Mixing materials can make them change.
- When a solid changes to a liquid it melts.
- When a liquid changes to a solid it freezes.
- Melting and freezing happen at different temperatures for different substances.
- Some changes can be reversed; others are irreversible.
- Materials can be separated in different ways.
- Sieving can separate mixtures of solids.
- Some materials cannot dissolve in a liquid; these are insoluble.
- Some materials can dissolve in a liquid; these are **soluble**.
- Insoluble solids can be separated from liquids by sieving or filtering.
- Soluble materials can be separated from liquids by evaporation.

Find out more about ...

Materials and their Properties

- how water is recycled.

Check-up

Callum and Josh have accidentally mixed rice, salt and flour together. They want to separate them again. What should they do?

The answer!

Do you remember the question about the polluted river? Even though water may look clean and clear, it may have chemicals dissolved in it that we can't see. Although the children have removed the rubbish, they have not been able to remove the dissolved chemicals in the water. If we stop dumping chemicals in rivers, eventually they will become clean.

4E Friction

What do you know?

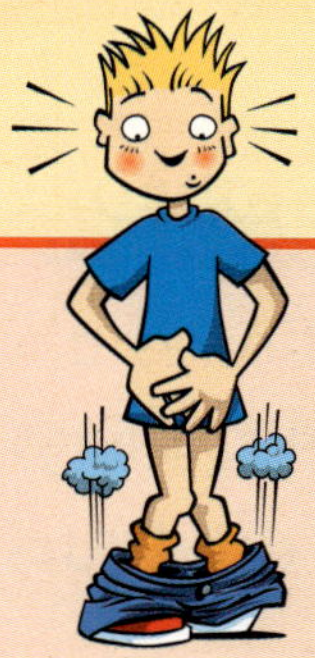

- Forces are pushes and pulls.
- We measure forces in newtons (N).
- Forces act in particular directions.
- We can't always see forces but we can measure them and observe what they do.
- Forces can make objects move or stop, and change speed, direction or even shape.
- **Friction** is a force that slows things down.

Friction happens when two surfaces move against each other. It lets us walk without slipping and sliding. It's the reason things don't slip out of our hands. It's even the reason our pants stay up! Without friction, the waistband of our pants would not grip our body!

Skills check

Can you …

- make careful observations and measurements?
- collect evidence and see how good it is?
- use your evidence to explain what you've found out?
- use your evidence to predict?

Words to learn

air resistance
forcemeter
friction
lubricant
lubrication
streamlined
streamlining
surface area
water resistance

Let's find out …

Claire's grandad slipped on his bathroom floor tiles. He wasn't hurt but he wanted his home to be made more safe for him. Claire and her mum are changing things in the bathroom and kitchen so that nothing will be too slippery. What changes could they make?

What is friction?

Things to learn

- Friction is a force that slows down moving things.
- We use **lubricants** to overcome friction.

Get a grip

Friction is caused by two surfaces moving against each other. As one surface passes over the other they grip. This slows the movement down. If the surface area is very big or the surfaces are very similar, there will be more friction and things will move very slowly.

Science friction

Even surfaces we think are perfectly smooth have a rough surface. If we look at them through a powerful microscope we can see troughs and ridges. These troughs and ridges catch against each other and slow things down.

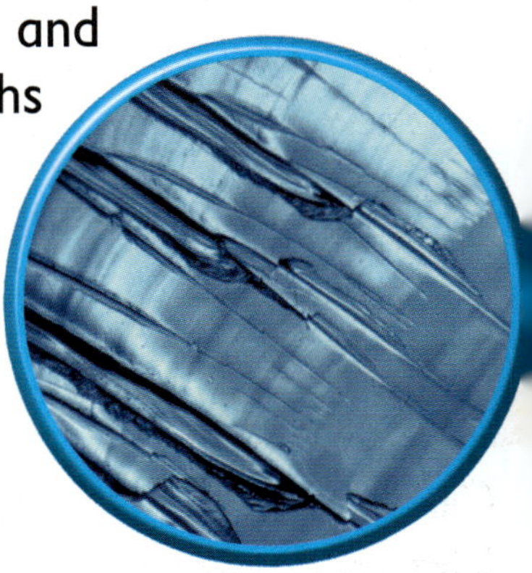

Slipping and sliding

Friction helps us to walk. If our feet didn't grip the floo we'd slip as if we were walking on ice. Have you ever slid across a polished floor in your socks? Is it easier or harder than sliding with trainers on? Shoes have a textured sole, called a 'tread', to stop you sliding.

Wheels have treads too. The tyres on a mountain bik or the caterpillar tracks on a digger have deep treads to grip on rough ground.

Skate away

Sledges need to slide across the snow easily. They have narrow runners to reduce the surface in contact with the snow. Skiers put wax on their skis to reduce the friction and make them ski faster.

Things to do

Hot stuff!

Lots of friction causes heat. Campers know that the friction caused by rubbing two sticks together can sometimes cause enough heat to light a fire.

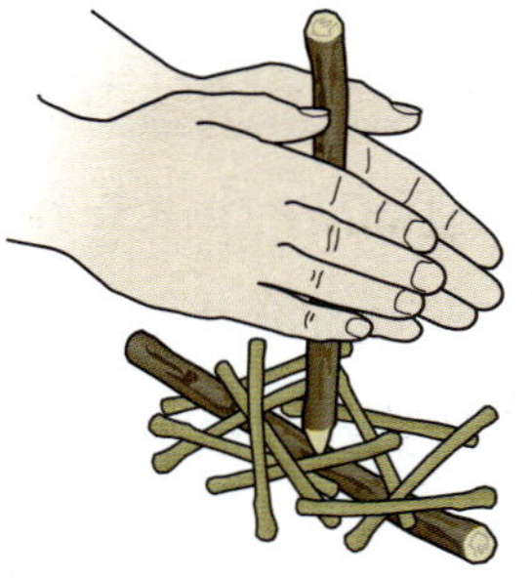

- Rub your hands together really quickly. The friction between your palms should create quite a bit of heat. Now do it under a running tap. What happens? Why do you think this is?

Wacky wobblers

- Put cubes of jelly in a bowl. Using only two fingers, see how many cubes you can move to another bowl in a minute. Now add some cooking oil to the cubes and try to move them back. How many can you move in a minute this time?

Wipe up any spilt oil or jelly from the floor to avoid an accident.

Exploring

Forces and motion
friction

Oil and water are both examples of lubricants. We use lubrication to reduce friction between moving surfaces.

Find out:

- where friction is useful or a nuisance and how we can reduce friction.

Did you know?

- Polar bears have fur on the soles of their feet to help them grip the ice.
- Watchmakers use tiny 'jewels' to reduce friction between the moving parts in watches.

I wonder ...

Why do the brakes on your bike work better on a dry day than on a wet one?

Measuring forces

Your challenge

- Find how much force is needed to move an object across a surface.
- Plan a fair test.
- Measure and record forces in newtons.

Claire watched her brother pull his toy truck. The more blocks he put in his truck the harder it was to make it move. Claire wondered why this was? She decided to investigate ...

What to do

Claire found an empty margarine tub and tied it to a forcemeter. She put the tub on the kitchen table and gently pulled on the forcemeter until the tub moved. She wrote down the force needed to make the tub move.

Claire added five marbles to the tub to make it heavier. Each time she added more marbles, she noted how much force was needed to move the tub.

What you need

- a plastic tub
- string
- a forcemeter
- several masses or marbles
- several surfaces, such as wood, card, carpet, sandpaper, plastic

What to check

Now try it yourselves.

- Claire measured the force when the tub fi
  started to move. Will you do the same?
- What surface will you do the experiment c
- Use a forcemeter if you have one.
- What do you think will happen?

What did you find?

Claire made a table of her results. It looked like this.

Number of marbles	Force needed to start tub moving (N)
0 (empty)	0·2
5	1.2
10	2·2
15	3·2
20	4·2
25	5·2
30	6·2
35	7·2

Claire noticed that with more marbles in the tub, the reading on her forcemeter was higher. She thought that a heavier tub needed more force to start it moving along the surface of the table.

- Use a spreadsheet to record your results then plot them on a line graph. Put the number of marbles or the mass on the x-axis and the force needed to move it on the y-axis.

Can you do better?

How good is your evidence? Can you make a general rule about your results?

Now predict

- What do you think would happen if Claire changed the container she used? Does the size of the container make a difference to how much force is needed to move it?
- Do you think her results would be different if she did the experiment on the carpet? Why?
- Claire took a few things out of the tub. What do you think happened?

Slippery surfaces

Your challenge

- Find out which surface is the most slippery.

What to do

The children in Mr Duffy's class were having a race. They decided to find out what would be the best racing surface. They had to decide what to measure, and how to record their results. Look at what the children thought. What do you think?

What you need

- a wooden block to act as your vehicle
- a ramp or plank
- materials to cover your plank's surface: carpet, card, bubble wrap, rubber, foil
- a metre ruler
- books or bricks to support the end of the plank

What to check

Now try it yourselves.

- What are you going to measure
- Is it fair?
- Are you only changing one thing
- What do you think will happen?

What did you find?

The children stopped adding bricks when the wooden block first began to slip down the slope.

They changed the surface of the slope and repeated their experiment using the same wooden block. They recorded their results in a table.

Surface of ramp	Height in bricks before the block moved
wood	3
card	2
carpet	4
felt	5
sandpaper	2

- Make a chart of your results. Use a computer program to help you.
- Which was the stickiest surface? Which was the slippiest? Why do you think that was?

Can you do better?

How good is your evidence?

What would happen if you lubricated the ramp? What would you use?

Now predict

Mr Duffy decided to have a 'Snail Grand Prix'. He gave a prize to the car that reached the finish line last on a tilted ramp. The children could use any surface to cover the ramp and the tyres on the toy cars.

- What do you think the children chose for the ramp and tyres? What do you think the winning car had on its tyres?
- If you have a light gate for your computer, use it to check which car moved first.

Different forces

Things to learn

- Friction is a force that exists between moving surfaces.
- Friction exists in liquids and gases too.
- Air resistance is a force that slows objects moving through air.
- Water resistance is a force that slows objects moving through water.

Forces all around

We live at the bottom of a sea of air. We are surrounded by invisible air. It presses down on us all the time. We can feel its force when the wind blows or when we move through it. We call this force **air resistance**.

Slowing down

A parachute slows down as it falls through the air. The air rubs against the parachute and slows it down. A parachute with a big canopy will fall slower than one with a small canopy. This is because there is a bigger **surface area** in contact with the air and so there is more air resistance.

Dolphins have beautifully streamlined bodies that cut quickly through the water

Streamlined shapes

Objects that have large, square or flat shapes meet a lot of resistance in water. Fish and marine mammals have pointed, slim shaped bodies to cut through the water. Their shapes reduce the **water resistance** that slows them down. We call these shapes **streamlined**. Streamlining is important in air too. The fastest sports cars have narrow, pointed, streamlined shapes. The air passes quickly over them and reduces the amount of air resistance.

Things to do

Fly a kite

- Make some different-shaped kites and fly them on a windy day. Which kites are the easiest to control? What difference does the size of the kite make? Can you feel how hard you have to pull on your kite against the air pushing it up?

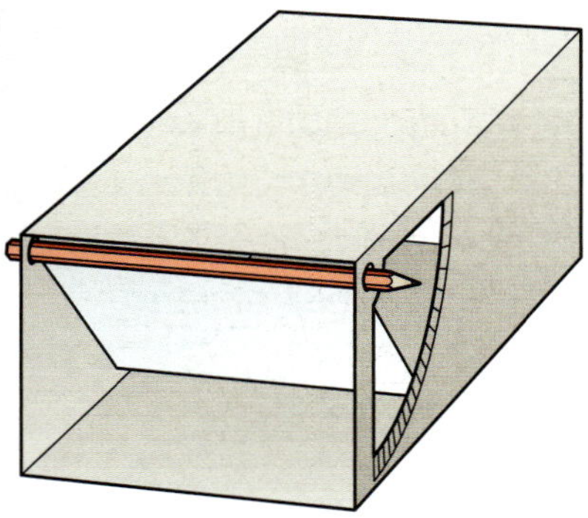

Windy weather

Sailors need to know the strength of the wind to help them sail.

- Find out about Admiral Beaufort and his wind scale.
- Make a 'wind gauge' to measure the force of the wind. Are your results the same as the local weather forecast?

Exploring

Forces and motion
Resistance and streamlining

Find out:

- more about friction in air and water.
- how parachutes work. Try the investigation 'Falling down'.

Did you know?

- The first kites were made 3000 years ago in China from silk and bamboo.
- In June 2000 a skydiver made a two-mile-high parachute jump using a triangular-shaped parachute invented in 1485! Lots of scientists thought it wouldn't work but it glided to Earth quite safely!

I wonder ...

Why are submarines torpedo-shaped and not cubes or spheres?

Testing spinners

Your challenge

- Find out which is the best spinner.

What to do

Cut out your spinner. Think about all of the ways you could change it.

You could try all of these – or can you think of something else?

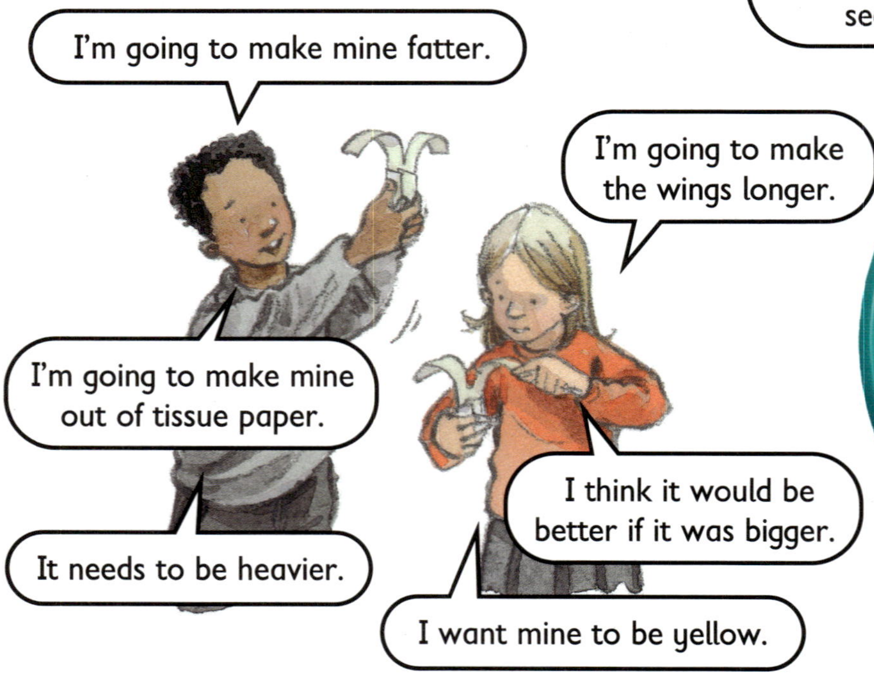

What you need

- spinner template
- scissors
- different sorts of paper
- paper clips
- a stopwatch or seconds timer
- a measuring tape

What to check

Now try it yourselves.

- What are you going to keep the same?
- What are you going to change?
- What are you going to measure or observe?
- How are you going to keep the test fair
- What do you think will happen?

What did you find?

The children changed the paper the spinner was made from. They thought that the slower it fell, the 'better' it was. They dropped their spinners from the same height each time. They measured how long they took to hit the ground. The children drew a table of their results:

Spinner material	Time taken (seconds)
writing paper	3.2
tissue paper	2.0
thin card	1.5
newspaper	3.6
magazine paper	4.4

The children weren't sure that they were using the best materials to make spinners. They noticed that the tissue paper spinner collapsed. They thought that maybe that wasn't fair. When they tried the magazine paper, their teacher walked past and made a draught. Maybe that wasn't fair?

- Can you tell the children where they went wrong with their experiment?

Can you do better?

What would you do if your results didn't seem quite right?

Now predict

- What other ways could the children test their spinners? Would the results be the same if they added paper clips to the spinners to make them heavier? What would happen if they dropped them from a higher place? Do you think the size of the spinner matters? Why?
- What is it about sycamore seeds that makes them spread everywhere?

Investigating friction

Your challenge

- Find out which shapes are the most streamlined.

What to do

Decide what you're going to measure and how you'll record your results. Here's what Stephan said to Oliver. What do you think?

What you need

- a long tube or plastic pop bottle with the top cut off
- very small pieces of plasticine – all the same size
- wallpaper paste or clear liquid soap
- thread
- a stopwatch or seconds timer

What to check

Now try it yourselves.

- What are you going to measure?
- How many times will you repeat the experiment?
- Why is this a good idea?
- What shapes will you try?
- How will you keep the test fair?
- What do you think will happen?

What did you find?

The boys tested the idea by timing how long it took different plasticine shapes to fall to the bottom of a bottle of paste. This is the table of their results.

Shape of plasticine	Time taken (seconds)
flat square	2·3
dome	2·6
sphere	1·9
sausage	1·5
torpedo	1·7

- Make a chart of your results. Use a computer program to help you.
- If you have a video recorder, record your results.
- Make a PowerPoint presentation of your experiment.

Can you do better?

How good is your evidence?

What would you do differently if you did this experiment again?

Now predict

The boys made sure all of the plasticine pieces weighed the same but they were surprised by their results. They thought the torpedo shape would be quickest.

- Why do you think they were wrong? Why do you think the dome shape was the slowest? Can you think of any other shapes to try?

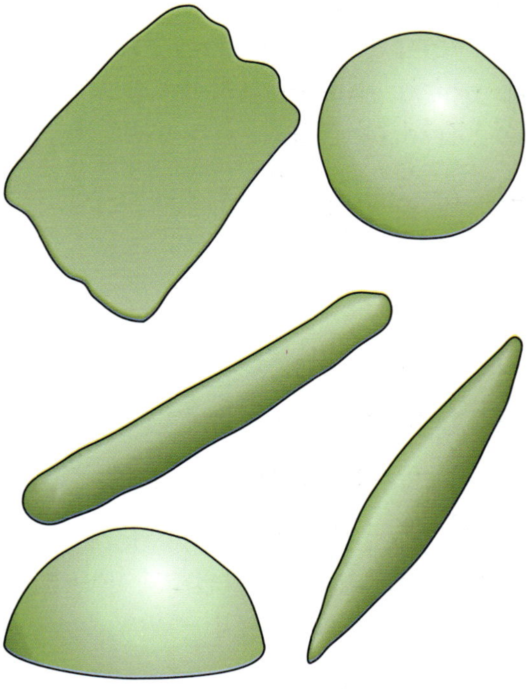

4E Review

What have you learned?

- Friction is a force that slows moving objects down.
- Lubrication reduces friction between solid surfaces.
- Air resistance is a force that slows things moving in air.
- Water resistance is a force that slows things moving in water.
- Streamlined shapes can reduce air and water resistance.

Find out more about ...

Physical processes

- why the space shuttle gets so hot as it re-enters the Earth's atmosphere.
- why the spaceshuttle doesn't get hot as it travels through outer space.
- how the space shuttle is slowed down as it lands.

Check-up

Anna is competing in an endurance bike race. She has to ride round and round a track for five miles! She is very fit and knows that she will be able to keep going. But she thinks that air resistance might slow her down.

- What should she wear to cut down the air resistance?

The answer!

Do you remember the question about Claire's grandad? Smooth surfaces, particularly when they are lubricated with something like water, can become very slippery and dangerous. Claire's grandad can increase the friction by keeping the surfaces dry. He could also use low friction materials such as rubber mats to help increase his grip.

4F Circuits and conductors

What do you know?

- Electrical items use either mains electricity or batteries.
- Electricity won't flow unless there is a complete **circuit**.
- The names of things – components – you can use in a simple circuit.
- Mains electricity can be dangerous if you don't use it properly.

When you go home you might turn on the lights, have a shower, dry your hair with a hair dryer, watch television or play a computer game. You might take something out of the fridge and warm it up in the microwave. We sometimes take electricity for granted. Without electricity, few of these things would be possible. Think what your world would be like without it!

Skills check

Can you …

- make careful observations and measurements?
- collect evidence and decide how good it is?
- use your evidence to explain what you found out?

Words to learn

battery
bulb
buzzer
break
circuit
conductivity
conductor
current
electrical
insulator
motor
switch
voltage

Let's find out …

Has your home got a hallway? Maybe there is a light on the landing. You can switch it on from the bottom of the stairs – and switch it off when you get to the top. One lamp, two switches, and only one source of electricity. How can that work?

Simple circuits

Things to learn

- A circuit needs a source of electricity.
- A complete circuit is needed for a device to work.
- Some materials conduct electricity and others do not.

It's electrifying!

Electricity is a very useful form of energy. It can be changed into other types of energy like light, heat and movement. It flows along wires that can be twisted to go anywhere. Imagine if your television worked on gas. You would need a gas pipe to it!

Everything in the world is made up of tiny particles called atoms. If we looked at an atom through a really powerful microscope we would see that it contained even smaller particles called electrons. Electrons move from one atom to another. This moving stream of electrons creates an electric **current**.

Round and round

A circuit is the path electricity takes when it flows. Electricity cannot (usually) jump gaps. The different components in the circuit must all be connected to each other to make a complete circuit. This is needed for electricity to flow. If your bike chain had any breaks in it, it wouldn't be able to move round in a circle and turn the wheels.

Making it work

Electricity comes from a source. The source might be a **battery** or 'mains' electricity from a socket in the wall. A battery acts like a pump. It provides the 'push' to drive the electrons round the circuit. Mains electricity has a much bigger push and can be very dangerous. Never play with mains electricity.

Things to do

Build a battery

Chemicals in a battery get together and push electrons round a complete circuit. An Italian scientist called Alessandro Volta invented the first battery in the eighteenth century. His 'Voltaic pile' was made by stacking up discs of zinc, copper and cloth soaked in salt water.

- Make a Voltaic pile with discs of aluminium foil, copper coins and circles of blotting paper soaked in salty water. Attach a wire to a copper coin and build up layers of foil, paper and coins. End with a wire attached to a foil disc.

Baffling batteries

Batteries come in many shapes and sizes. How many can you find? All batteries are marked with a **+** and a **–**. These are the positive (+) and negative (–) **terminals** of the battery. Electricity flows from the negative terminal of the battery to the positive terminal.

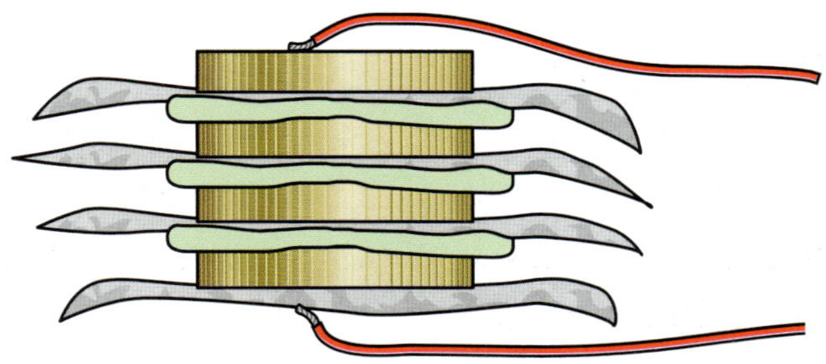

Digging deeper

Physical processes
Michael Faraday

Find out:

- about the electrical genius Michael Faraday and how his discoveries changed the world.

Did you know?

- The American inventor, Benjamin Franklin, proved that lightning is a form of electricity in a very dangerous way. He flew a kite into a thundercloud. Electricity flowed down the damp kite string and into a key at the end of it. When Franklin put his finger near the key it produced a spark. Don't try this yourself – Franklin was very lucky! The next person who tried this was killed!

I wonder …

Why is a fire-fighter's helmet made of fibreglass and not metal? Why do electricians use wooden ladders?

Investigating circuits

Your challenge

- Find out how to make a **bulb** light up.

What to do

- Decide how to connect up your circuit. Try to make your bulb light with just one wire.
- Do you need a bulb holder? Does it matter which way round the battery is?

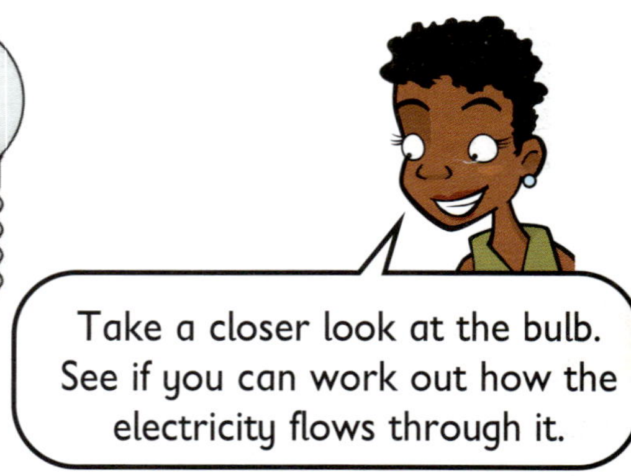

What you need

- batteries
- bulbs and holders
- wires
- a magnifying glass or hand lens

What to check

Now try it yourselves.

- How can you make your bulb light in more than one way?
- If your circuit isn't working, what will you check?
- How will you record your investigation?

What did you find?

The children drew diagrams of their results. Some of their circuits worked but others didn't.

- Look at their diagrams. Decide which bulbs would light and which ones wouldn't.
- What is alike about circuits that work?

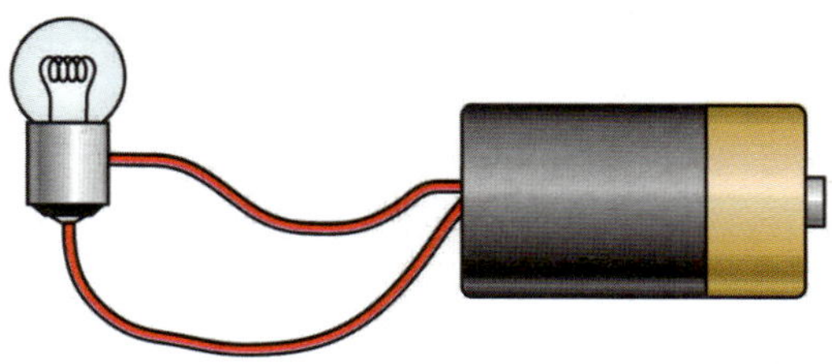

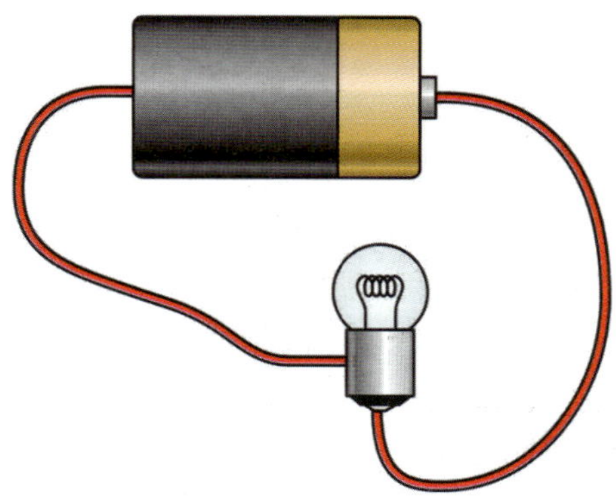

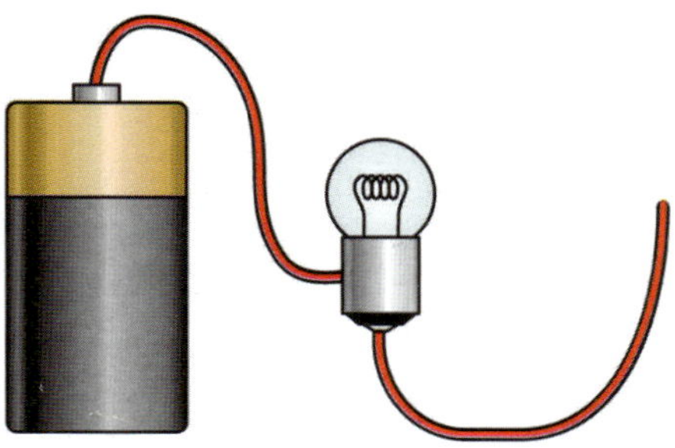

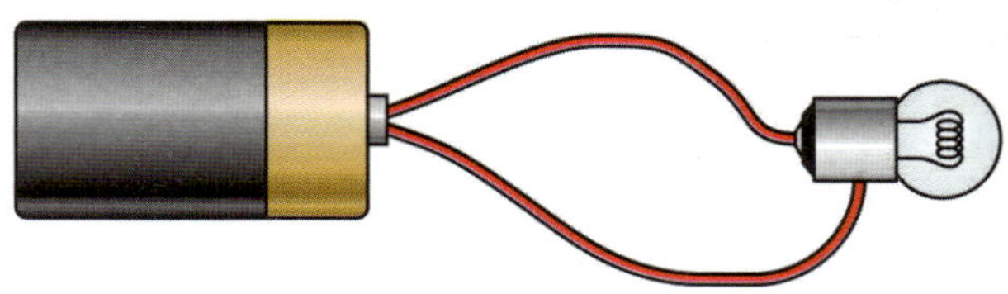

Can you do better?

Make up a rule that must be followed to make a circuit work.

Ask your friends to make a circuit from the diagram you drew.

Now predict

- A torch usually has more than one battery inside it. How would you draw a circuit diagram for a torch?

Conductors and insulators

Your challenge

- Find out which materials **conduct** electricity.

What to do

Make a circuit with a **break** in it, like this:

We call this sort of circuit an open circuit. Put some test materials in the gap. If the bulb lights up, you have made a complete circuit. Your material is an electrical **conductor**. Electricity flows easily through an electrical conductor. If the bulb doesn't light up, you have tested an electrical insulator. The electricity will not flow easily through an electrical insulator.

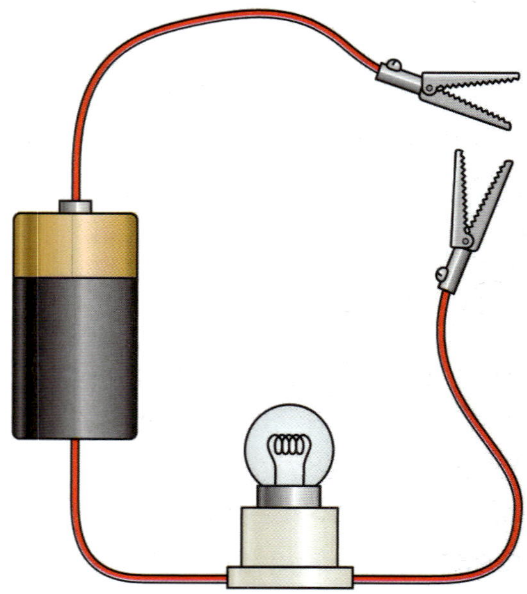

Don't test watches or anything electrical!

What you need

- a battery
- a bulb or buzzer
- three wires
- a selection of materials to test
- a pencil, sharpened at both ends

What to check

Now try each material yourselves.

- Predict what materials will be conductors.

What did you find?

This chart shows Hannah's predictions:

Materials	Conductor? Yes/no
metal paper clip	yes
birthday card	no
pencil eraser	no
plastic toothbrush	no
steel scissors	yes
silver necklace	yes
aluminium foil	yes

Hannah predicted the results of her tests correctly.

- Use your own results or Hannah's. Make a general rule about materials that are good conductors and those that are not.
- Make a list of where we use electrical conductors and insulators at home and at school.
- Why is it important to insulate electrical wire?

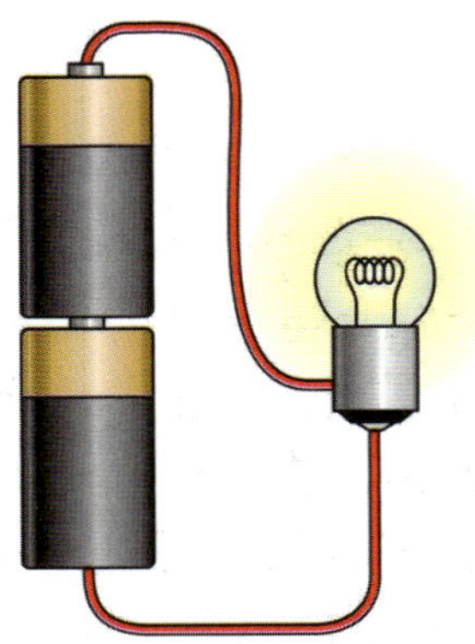

Can you do better?

Now test the pencil 'lead' – not real lead, but a material called carbon. What do you notice about the brightness of your bulb? What difference does this make to your general rule?

Now predict

The wooden part of the pencil is an insulator. The pencil lead is a conductor. Not a good conductor – but still a conductor.

- Try pencils of different lengths. What do you think is happening?

Switches and batteries

Things to learn

- A switch can be used to make or break a circuit.
- Voltage is the amount of 'push' in a circuit.
- Adding batteries to a circuit changes the voltage in it.

Switching on

A **switch** is a gap in a circuit that can be opened and closed. When the switch is open the circuit is broken. Electricity cannot flow. When the switch is closed, the circuit is complete and the electric current can flow. The switch works whatever else is in the circuit. What materials are switches made from? Why?

Various voltages

The amount of 'push' in a circuit or battery is called the **voltage**. It's named after the inventor Alessandro Volta. If you look at a battery, the number printed on the sides is the voltage. We measure voltage in volts (V). The most common batteries are made of zinc and carbon. They have a voltage of 1·5 V or 3 V or 4·5 V and so on.

The 12 V battery used in cars can produce a much stronger push than a torch battery. It can make you jump!

Mains electricity at 240 V has a much bigger push than a battery. Mains electricity can power large machinery. But it can also kill.

Match it up

When you make your own circuits, match the voltage of your batteries to the other components in the circuit. A 1·5 V battery and a 1·5 V bulb will work well. If you add two more batteries you'll increase the voltage to 4·5 V and blow your 1·5 V bulb!

Things to do

Morse messages

Samuel Morse invented the Morse Code to help send messages by electric telegraph. The Morse 'key' is a special kind of switch. Pressing it makes a series of short beeps (dots) and longer beeps (dashes). These represent letters of the alphabet and so make words.

- Make your own telegraph with a **buzzer** and a push switch. Send a message to your friend.

Digging deeper

Electricity and magnetism
Power supply

Find out:

- about different types of electricity generation.
- how electricity reaches us in our homes.
- what a transformer is and why it is important.

Did you know?

- Cragside House in Northumberland was the first house in the world to be lit by electricity. The electric lamps had to be switched on by putting them in a dish of mercury.
- Both Joseph Swan of Newcastle and the American, Thomas Alva Edison, invented the light bulb around the same time – 1879.

I wonder ...

Why is a bathroom light switch on a cord? All the other switches in the house are plastic and fixed to the wall!

Designing switches

Your challenge

- Design a switch to operate components in a circuit.

Rohan's mum works at home. She has an office with no windows, which sometimes causes problems.

What to do

Rohan built his mum a rain detector alarm. It looked like this:

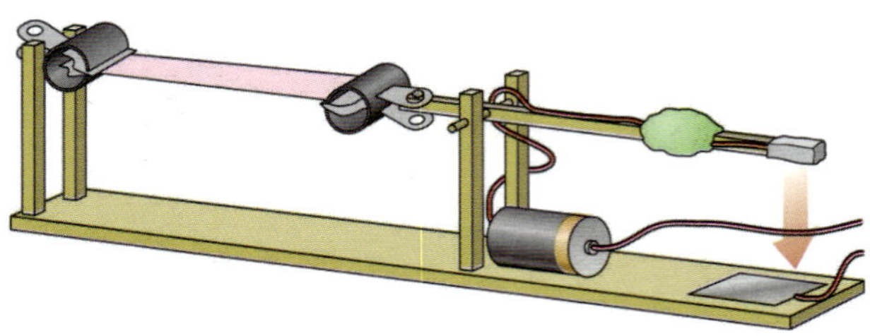

When it rained, the tissue paper got wet and tore apart. This made the see-saw arm fall onto a piece of cooking foil. The circuit was complete and a buzzer sounded in his mum's office.

You could build a rain detector or use an interesting switch to control a circuit for something else. Here are some ideas.

What you need

- wires
- a motor
- buzzers
- foil
- balsa wood
- split pins
- bulbs
- batteries
- a selection of junk modelling materials

What to check

Now try it yourselves.

- Where will you put your switch?
- Does it matter where it goes in the circuit?
- What do you think will happen?

What did you find?

Rohan investigated different types of switches. Here are some of them.

- How do you think they work?
- Where do you think they are used?
- What do they control?

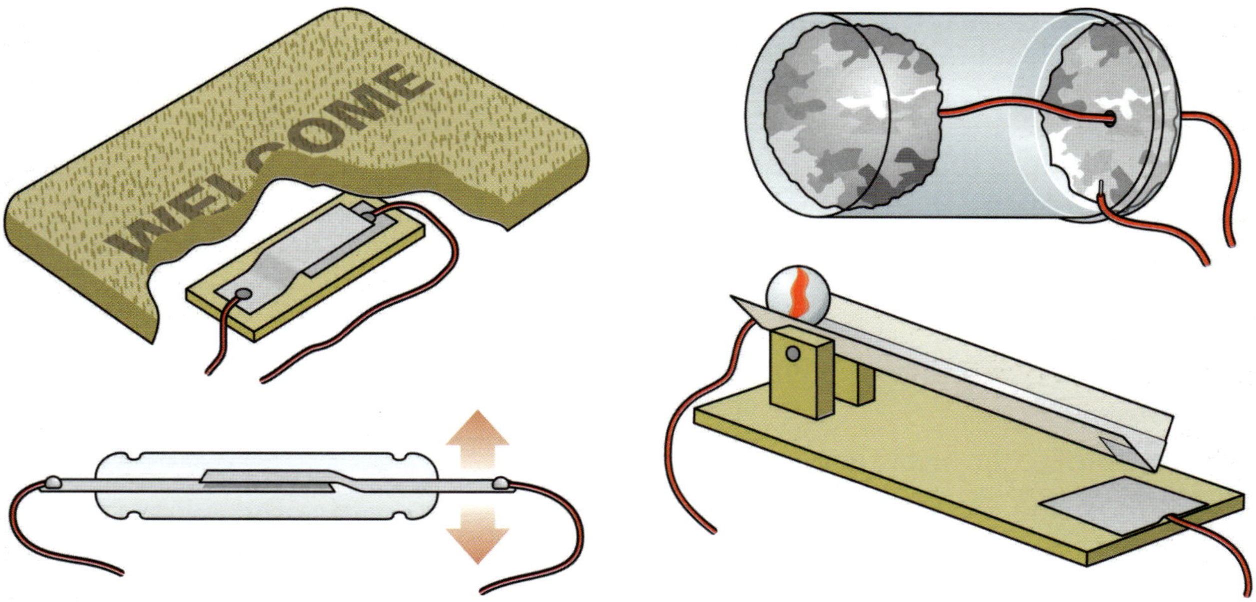

Can you do better?

Some switches are on/off switches. Some switches need pressing to keep them on.
Draw a diagram of a circuit with the best switch so that someone else could build it.
Why is this the best switch for the job?

Now predict

Georgia loves to read but her mum is always telling her off! She enjoys her stories so much that she doesn't notice when it starts to get dark. Georgia's mum is worried that she'll hurt her eyes.

- What can she build to switch the light on as it gets darker? You could use a computer and a light sensor to help you.

Brighter bulbs

Your challenge

- Alter the brightness of a bulb in a circuit.
- Alter the volume of a buzzer in a circuit.
- Alter the speed of a motor in a circuit.
- Plan a fair test.

Molly has made a model car. It has two bulbs for headlights and a buzzer for the horn, all powered by a battery.

What to do

How can Molly get brighter bulbs? How can she make her buzzer work well? Make up a circuit. What will you change?

Decide what you will observe or measure. Remember to make only one change at a time. You could use these ideas. Or think of a change of your own.

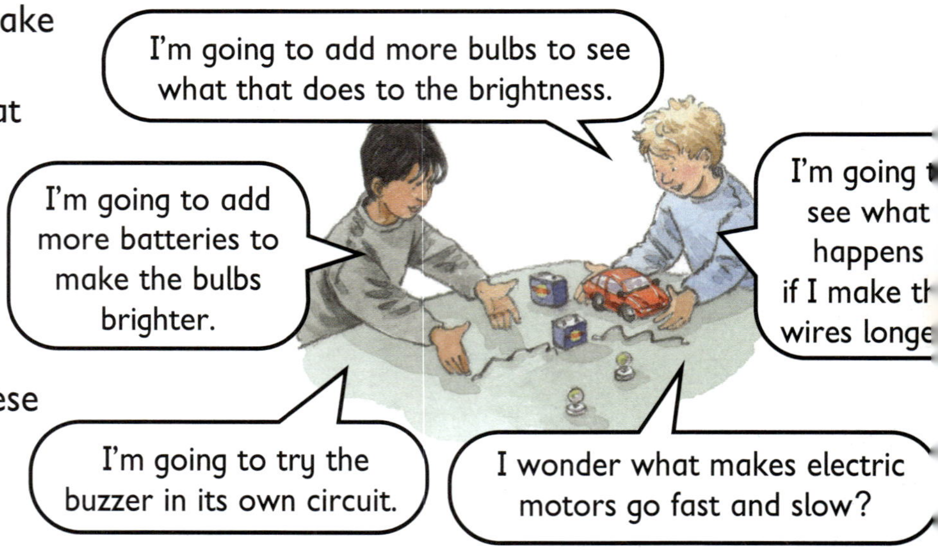

What you need

- batteries
- bulbs
- a buzzer
- an electric motor
- connecting wires
- a light sensor

What to check

Now try it yourselves.

- Don't add too many batteries at once! You will blow the bulb.
- How will you judge how bright the bulbs are or how loud a buzzer is?
- How will you record your results?

What did you find?

Molly decided to use two batteries in a circuit and to keep adding bulbs to see what happened. She put her results in a table.

Number of bulbs	Brightness
1	extremely bright
2	bright
3	dim
4	very dim
5	can't see any light

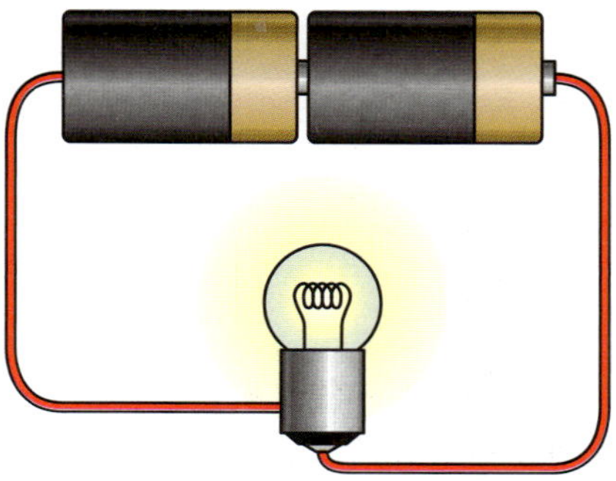

- Draw a chart of your results or use Molly's. If you have a light sensor on your computer use it to make more accurate measurements. You could plot these results on a bar graph.
- When were the bulbs brightest? When were they dimmest? Why do you think that was? Were all the bulbs in the circuit equally dim or equally bright? Why was that?

Can you do better?

Why should you only make one change at a time?

Did you ever make more than one change? What's wrong with that?

Now predict

Molly had space to put two batteries in her model. She connected the bulbs to them and was happy with how bright they were. When she connected the buzzer the lights went dimmer again. The buzzer worked all the time the lights were on.

- How can Molly have two bright bulbs and a buzzer she can turn on and off using just two batteries?
- How can Molly make an electric motor go faster and slower?

4F Review

What have you learned?

- You know the difference between electricity from batteries and mains electricity.
- You can construct a simple circuit.
- You can say why some simple circuits will work and others will not.
- You know what an electrical conductor is and you can name some.
- You know what an electrical insulator is and you can name some.
- You know how electricity travels in a circuit.
- You can construct a switch.
- You can explain how to change the brightness of bulbs, the speed of a motor or the volume of a buzzer in a circuit.
- You can describe what might happen in a circuit if the components are not matched.

Find out more about ...

- how a bicycle can generate electricity.
- how a dimmer switch works.

Check-up

Sophie has made a circuit using two batteries, a bulb and a motor but it doesn't work.

Think of as many reasons as you can to explain why the circuit might not work.

The answer!

Remember that light on the landing? Do you switch it on to go downstairs on a dark morning? Do you turn it off before you go out? How does that work? Well, you only need one source of electricity. But those two switches need to be in separate circuits. The electricity needs two different paths to the bulb. Try it with a bulb, a battery and two switches. How can you make it work?

4A Moving and growing checklist

What do you know?

Think about these statements.

Which do you know? Which can you do?

- I can name parts of my body – knee, elbow, wrist, thigh etc.
- I can tell you what I observe when I do things.
- I know that bones grow as an animal grows.
- I can make observations about which bones are biggest.
- I can group bones by size.
- I can make observations about how bone feels and looks.
- I know why we have a skeleton and muscles.
- I can explain why muscles change shape as I move.
- I can measure the length of people's limbs.
- I can explain how joints work.
- I know where my heart is in my body and what it does.
- I know that muscles work in pairs: when one muscle contracts the other relaxes.
- I know that when I investigate I can only change one factor at a time – the people I measure, for example.
- I can relate my conclusion to my prediction and use scientific language.

4B Habitats checklist

What do you know?

Think about these statements.

Which do you know? Which can you do?

- I can describe my animal or plant.
- I can tell you what I observe.
- I can tell you the conditions that animals and plants need to survive.
- I can say that different animals and plants are found in different places.
- I can place animals and plants into groups.
- I can make and record regular observations of my habitats.
- I can explain how an animal, like a fish or a penguin, is adapted to its environment.
- I can explain why an animal or plant has adapted to suit its environment.
- I can explain why woodlice chose similar places in my investigation.
- I can use a branching key to identify animals and plants.
- I can use a branching key to group animals or plants, with good reasons.
- I can use a food chain to describe a feeding relationship.
- I can suggest ways I could improve my habitat investigations.

4C Keeping warm checklist

What do you know?

Think about these statements.

Which do you know? Which can you do?

- I can describe an object such as a thermal insulator.
- I can tell you what I observe.
- I can identify a range of materials, like wood, plastic and metal.
- I can group materials on how good they are as thermal insulators.
- I can make and record regular observations of cooling and warming.
- I can use a stopwatch.
- I know that saucepans are made from a conductor and the handle is made from an insulator.
- I can explain which insulation type keeps water warmest and ice coldest.
- I can measure temperature accurately.
- I know that metals are good electrical and thermal conductors.
- I know that a hot drink will cool to room temperature if left.
- I can keep my investigations fair, by only changing one factor at a time.
- I can plot a bar chart of my results.

4D Separating solids and liquids checklist

What do you know?

Think about these statements.

Which do you know? Which can you do?

- I can explain the differences between ice and water.
- I can list some differences between solids and liquids, and give you some examples.
- I can sort familiar materials into solids and liquids and give you reasons.
- I can tell you what happens to ice if you heat it, or water if you cool it.
- I can sort unfamiliar materials into groups and give you reasons for my decisions.
- I know that changes to ice and water can be reversed.
- I know how sieves work, and can explain how a filter is like a fine sieve.
- I can tell you how the differences between materials can be used to group them as solids or liquids.
- I can explain filtering and evaporation.

4E Friction checklist

What do you know?

Think about these statements.

Which do you know? Which can you do?

- I can make observations of the way things move.
- I can describe the effects of friction on something I am trying to move.
- I can compare the test results for two or more moving objects.
- I can compare differences in frictional forces – for example, how something moves over different surfaces.
- I can make measurements using a newtonmeter.
- I can explain how different conditions lead to different frictional effects – for example, how rougher surfaces can slow something down.
- I can graph my scientific enquiry results.
- I can explain my scientific enquiry results from what I know about friction.
- I can make a general statement – heavier spinners fall faster, pointed shapes travel faster through water.

4F Circuits and conductors checklist

What do you know?

Think about these statements.

Which do you know? Which can you do?

- I can show you how to make a simple circuit, either by talking to you or by drawing a picture.
- I can make up a simple circuit and explain what I have done.
- I can use electrical components to make up simple circuits and tell you whether my predictions about them were correct.
- I can compare the way that bulbs work in different electrical circuits.
- I can carry out a fair test – of insulators and conductors, or of changes in an electrical circuit – and suggest ways of doing it better.
- I can explain to you why a bulb does not light – that there is a break in the circuit or that the switch is open.
- I can choose components to add to my circuits, predict what they will do, and explain what happened when I added them.
- I can tell you how to put a buzzer or motor into an electric circuit, and how to control it with a switch.

Glossary

adapted – an animal or a plant that has changed to suit its environment
air resistance – a friction force that slows down objects moving through the air
backbone – the long bone in the back made up of several smaller bones
battery – pushes electricity round a circuit
break – gap in a circuit
bulb – contains a fine wire that glows to emit light
buzzer – vibrates noisily
Celsius – a temperature scale
circuit – path of electricity
classification – sorting things into specific groups
condition – the state in which animals and plants live
conduct – transmit heat, sound or electricity
conductor – a material that transmits heat, sound or electricity easily
consumer – an animal or a plant that eats other animals or plants
contract – becoming smaller or shorter
current – the electricity that flows round a circuit
degree – a unit of temperature
dissolve – when a solid mixes with a liquid and the mixture looks clear
environment – our general surroundings
evolution – the process that has changed animals and plants over millions of years
external – outside a person, place or object
filtering – separating a solid from a liquid or gas by sieving it out
food chain – the link between plants and animals and what they eat
friction – a force between touching surfaces
gas – an air-like substance with a weight but no shape
habitat – the natural home of an animal or plant
insoluble – a solid that does not dissolve in a liquid
insulation – material that slows or stops heat, sound or electricity
internal – inside a person, place or object
key – a means to help identify something or someone
liquid – a material that flows into a container to make a flat surface
lubricant – something that reduces the friction between surfaces, like oil

mammal – an animal that gives birth to a live baby and feeds it young with milk from the mother's body

melt – to change from solid to liquid when warm

muscle – body tissue that can contract and pull – but not expand and push

particle – a very small piece of something

predator – an animal that eats another animal for food

prey – an animal that is eaten by a predator

producer – provides food for animals

protects – keeps safe from harm

relax – muscle not contracting and so getting bigger or longer

ribs – bony cage that protects the body organs and moves for breathing

shell – a hard protective covering

sieve – an instrument used to separate solids from liquids

skeleton – the framework of bones in your body

skull – bony protection for the brain

solid – a material that keeps its shape - however small

solidify – to become solid

soluble – a solid that dissolves in a liquid

solution – a liquid with something dissolved in it

streamlined – specially shaped to reduce resistance when travelling through air or water

surface area – the amount of space covered by something

switch – makes and breaks a circuit

temperature – measure of how hot something is

tendons – join the muscles to the bones at the joints

terminal – part of an electrical device through which electricity enters or leaves

thermal – involving heat

thermometer – instrument to measure temperature

vertebrate – a creature with a backbone

voltage – the force of an electrical current measured in volts

water resistance – a friction force that slows down objects moving through water

Randal Cremer Primary School
Ormsby Street
London E2 8JG
Tel: 020 7739 8162
Fax: 020 7729 5807